The
Everlasting Covenant

Content and Value of the Old Testament

HORACE R. WEAVER

GRADED PRESS

NASHVILLE

THE EVERLASTING COVENANT
CONTENT AND VALUE OF THE OLD TESTAMENT

Copyright © 1965 by Graded Press

Scripture quotations are from the Revised
Standard Version of the Bible, copyrighted
1946 and 1952 by the Division of Christian Education, National Council of
Churches, and are used by permission.

SET UP, PRINTED, AND BOUND BY THE
PARTHENON PRESS, AT NASHVILLE
TENNESSEE, UNITED STATES OF AMERICA

To my wife

Lenore

Contents

Prologue 7
Part I: The Historical Approach to Bible Study 11
  1. The Founding Fathers 13
  2. Moses: Prince of Egypt, Deliverer, and
     Covenant Maker 24
  3. The Conquest of Canaan—Period of the
     Judges—Monarchy 36
  4. The Two Kingdoms and Their Downfall 49
  5. The Postexilic Period 57
Part II: The Literature of the Old Testament 69
  1. Pre-Monarchic Literature 76
  2. The Literary Renaissance of the Monarchy 79
  3. The Literature of the Divided Kingdom 88
  4. The Literature of Judah in the Seventh
     Century B.C. 101
  5. The Literature of Judah in the Period of
     the Exile 113
  6. The Literature of Judah in the Persian and
     Greek Periods 123
Part III: God's Saving Action in History 148
  1. The Election of and Covenant With the Patriarchs 153
  2. God's Saving Action in Redeeming His Chosen
     People From Egypt 158
  3. Reinterpretations in the Days of the Conquest .. 173
  4. The Davidic Covenant: A New Covenant for
     Israel 181
  5. Prophecy and Deuteronomy 188
  6. Prophecies of a New Saving Act of God 198
  7. The Postexilic Response 205
*Epilogue: The Value of the Old Testament for
  Christians* 217
Appendix A 224
Appendix B 225
Index 227

Prologue

In READING THE Bible many adults are disturbed because of the diversity, rather than the unity, which they find. They recognize that the Bible was written during the long span of twelve to thirteen centuries. Customs, laws, political situations, religious rites, and theological understanding changed considerably during these centuries. Furthermore, even the languages used for recording the historic events were diverse—Hebrew, Aramaic, and Greek.

The average reader of the Bible notes other divergencies. He discovers that the Bible is a virtual library of various types of literature, such as legal codes, genealogies, narratives, history, poetry, novels, proverbs, letters, gospels, and apocalypses. Moreover, these divergent types of writings are also divergent types of channels through which God's will was made known. These channels were the priest with his Torah (instructions), the wise man with his counsel, and the prophet with his "word of the Lord."

Interestingly enough, God's will was revealed through all these different centuries, through the different types of literary forms, and through varied channels. Obviously some media were considered better than others, as for example, the prophet whose "thus says the Lord" replaced the priestly sacred lots (the Urim and the Thummim). Similarly the historical narratives of Genesis were valued more highly than Proverbs. Yet through them all ran a theme that united the centuries, the literature, and the varied channels together—the covenant.

The fundamental axiom of Israel's faith was the covenant with God. Underlying the covenant was the experience of Israel that God had chosen her. The experience of being elected "or chosen" by God preceded the experience of covenant. Grace preceded law. Gen. 12 and 15 relate the call (election) of Abraham and his seed and the three-

7

fold promises given to Abraham: to make of Abraham a great nation, to give his descendants the land of Canaan, and to bless all mankind through his offspring.

Abraham's covenant was reaffirmed and expanded in the days of Moses during the Exodus from Egypt, the crossing of the Reed Sea, and the wilderness experience at Sinai and Kadesh-barnea. Joshua reaffirmed the continuity of the promises at Shechem after winning the land of Canaan (Josh. 24).

The Israelites always looked back to the days when the mighty acts of God were evident in their national life. This backward look was based on their confidence that God was active in their historic life. Their faith was not a matter of concepts about the nature of God or of God's demands for man. Rather, it was centered in historical events. God's mode of revelation was in the historic events of their days. So Israel, through the centuries, had a special way of looking at history—for history was considered the arena of God's activity.

The early confessional creeds of Deut. 26:5-9 and Josh. 24 clearly presuppose that God is the Lord of history. So Israel's life found meaning and purpose because history had meaning and purpose. Furthermore, God had chosen Israel as the agency through whom his meaning and purpose were to be revealed to all mankind: Israel was to be a "light to the Gentiles." Israel's awareness of being called into special relationship with God originated with Abraham; it was renewed with Moses and Joshua; and finally a new covenant was made with David, the first great monarch. In each event God initiated the action; yet in each event Israel was called upon to respond in obedience to his will.

Biblical writers were concerned not so much in teaching a specific doctrine about God as in eliciting a right relationship with him. For this purpose both Old and New Testaments (covenants) were written. (We should think of a covenant not as a written document but as a relationship with God.)

Thus, we see that the unity amidst the diversity in the Bible is found in the experience of election and of covenant. The narratives and genealogies of Genesis; the poetry of the prophets and psalms; the legalism of Leviticus; the novels of Ruth and Jonah; the Gospels of Matthew, Mark, Luke, and John; and the letters of Paul, Peter, James, and John all presuppose the experience of being chosen by God, with its response of covenant. Such experiences affirm God's activity in the historical events of Israel's national life.

Each of the writers of the New Testament assumed that God acted anew in the life, death, and resurrection of Jesus Christ. They believed that he who had acted creatively and redemptively in ancient Israel's behalf acted again in Israel's life through the "anointed One" (the Messiah, that is, the Christ).

A careful reading of Paul's sermon as it appears in Acts 13:16-23 shows the basic unity of the two covenants (the Old and New Testaments) in Jews's experience of being chosen of God for a specific responsibility. Paul is portrayed as having recited the confessional creeds of the Jewish faith:

> The God of this people Israel chose our fathers and made the people great during their stay in the land of Egypt, and with uplifted arm he led them out of it. And for about forty years he bore with them in the wilderness . . . . he gave them their land [in Canaan] . . . . raised up David to be their king. . . . Of this man's posterity God has brought to Israel a Savior Jesus, as he promised.

(Compare Acts 13:16-23 with Deut. 26:5-9 and Josh. 24.) This passage clearly assumes the unity of the Old and New covenants to be God's choice of the people of Israel and the covenant made between them and God.

The New Testament writers, who based their thinking for the most part on Isa. 40–55, assumed the Christians (the called of Christ, God's anointed) were the New Israel. They were called by God to replace the sons of Abraham, who denied the covenant by not fulfilling God's purposes. They had experienced a *new* Exodus, a *new* redemption, a *new* law, a *new* life, a *new* sacrifice, a *new* hope in Christ. The third promise that all mankind would be blessed through the seed of Abraham was now being fulfilled through Christ. Thus Gentiles who accepted Christ's call to discipleship now formed the New Israel.

The organization of this text on the content and value of the Old Testament is in three parts: The first (Part I) aims to help the reader understand the history of Israel, God's chosen people, from the days of the patriarchs to the coming of Christ. The second (Part II) is designed to help the reader understand the literature of the Bible against the historical background of Israel and to see it in its proper chronological order. The third (Part III) is planned to help the reader understand the various ways in which the experience of being a "chosen people" was reinterpreted by succeeding generations as they attempted to make their faith relevant for their day. In this third area we shall see how the concept of covenant was reinterpreted by Moses, David, the prophets, Deuteronomy, the exiles in Babylonia, Nehemiah and Ezra, and the Chronicler. This suggests that we of the New Israel should be thinking in terms of reinterpretations too, even as our spiritual forefathers did before us. We need to rethink the meaning of election and covenant in order to make the ancient faith of our fathers relevant for our age.

As the writer of this text, I hope that the readers will fulfill that part of the objective of Christian education which seeks to help persons "to become aware of God . . . and to respond to him in faith and love."

Part I

THE HISTORICAL APPROACH
TO BIBLE STUDY

ONE OF THE MOST significant ways of understanding the Bible is to develop a sense of history. He who would understand Moses thoroughly, for example, should know the century in which he lived, what the social, political, aesthetic, and religious customs of his native land (Egypt) were. He would want to know something about the pharaoh who ruled the land, what his conception of kingship was like, what image he had of himself, what his moral, social, civil, and military habits were. In short, he would need to know the setting in which Moses lived.

As we seek to understand the history of Israel, we must distinguish between two approaches to history. The first approach is nontheological, that is, it understands history without any reference to God as a participant. "Pure" history (if, in fact, there can really be such) would describe the crossing of the Red Sea (or Reed Sea) under the leadership of Moses without considering the theological claim that God acted in Israel's behalf in the crossing. The second approach to history views all events of history as under the purpose and control of God, the Lord of history. It would describe the crossing of the Red Sea as under the providence and purposes of God.

The theological approach superimposes upon the events of history the claims of faith, whereas the first approach seeks the historic facts minus the interpretation. The second does not necessarily contradict the first! In fact, the theological interpretations are built on the raw data of history. The theological approach is often called salvation-history (*Heilsgeschichte* in German) : the other is simply called history.

We should note that every historian writes from some very definite and specific perspective. If he were an atheist (as a Marxist historian would be), he would not be able to include the theological claims of a Christian historian. Another historian may write from the conviction that geographical locations determine a people's actions and faith. The Christian theologian admittedly writes from his "bias," namely, that God is the Lord of history and that his actions in history were clearly seen by men of faith.

In Part III of this book we will study the theological approach (*Heilsgeschichte*) to history. It is perhaps the most significant way to study the Bible, for it is concerned with the "Mighty Acts of God" in history. It declares God's providence and his revelation to man (in both the past and the present) and calls for man's response to this encounter with the ever-present living God.

As significant as *Heilsgeschichte* is, we nonetheless need to develop a knowledge of the history (*Geschichte*) of Israel in its social, economic, political, military, and religious setting. This will give meaning and enlightenment to our understanding of God's action in history.

Our concern in Part I is to help the reader develop a knowledge of the outline of biblical history. For our purposes we will divide biblical history into five periods with the following titles: (a) The Founding Fathers (the Patriarchs) ; (b) Moses: Prince of Egypt, Deliverer, and Covenant Maker; (c) The Conquest of Canaan—Period of the Judges—and the Rise of the Monarchy; (d) The Two Kingdoms, and Their Downfall; (e) The Postexilic Period.

CHAPTER 1

The Founding Fathers

THE FATHERS (often called the patriarchs) who founded the faith of Israel include Abraham, Isaac, Jacob, and Joseph. Abraham is considered the father of the faith ("Abraham your father," Isa. 51:2). Until recently, Old Testament studies assumed that Abraham was not an individual. Rather the name "Abraham" was thought to represent a whole tribe or clan. Thus, when "Abraham" went to Beersheba, it meant that the clan (or tribe) bearing his name went to Beersheba. This identification of a clan with a particular name is what is meant when Abraham is called an eponymous hero. Recent insights from archaeological discoveries in the Near East have made it quite clear that the customs of the period in which the patriarchs are dated (about 2000–1600 B.C.) are accurately reflected in our biblical narratives; so much so that the tendency is to consider Abraham not only as an eponymous hero but as an individual too. We will follow this trend and consider Abraham as an individual person.

Let us turn our attention now to the historical setting of the patriarchs.

The Patriarchs: Abraham, Isaac, and Jacob

Archaeologists have thus far not been able to discover any records by or about the patriarchs in nonbiblical sources. However, we do know a great deal about the type of people they were, where they came from, the civilization of their day, their social customs, and their religious beliefs.

Though Abraham (called "Abram" prior to his making

a covenant with God, Gen. 17; but we shall use the fuller name in this study) may have been born in Ur, he spent most of his life at Haran, a major city of the Arameans. We shall take a look at Haran after noting the great influences that Ur may have exerted on the boy, Abraham.

THE INFLUENCES OF SUMER, AKKAD, AND NEO-SUMERIAN CIVILIZATIONS

Gen. 11:31 tells us that Abraham with his father, Terah, and his brother, Nahor, left Ur of the Chaldeans (Babylonia) and went to Haran. Scholars are of divided opinion as to whether Abraham lived in Ur. There is some question therefore as to how much influence Ur had on the life of the patriarch. However, since both Ur and Haran were influential cities in Mesopotamia in 2000 B.C. and later, since both were dominated by Semitic rulers, and since both were greatly influenced by Sumerian and Akkadian cultures, from them we can learn a great deal about the period in which Abraham lived.

During the twenty-sixth century B.C., Ur was the capital of the great kingdom of Sumer. The Sumerians dominated southern Mesopotamia (the land between the Tigris and Euphrates rivers) for a thousand years, until conquered in 2300 B.C. by a Semitic people, the Akkadians. Two centuries later the Sumerians rose to power again and these people, today remembered as neo-Sumerians, ruled the land until the time when the great Semitic ruler, Hammurabi, conquered the land. The Sumerian culture continued despite rule by the Akkadians.

The cultures of Sumer and Akkad lived on for centuries through the schools and academies. Sumerian language and literature were the bases for the entire educational system. Let us look at some evidences of the very highly developed culture.

In Sumer, political power was originally invested in the hands of free citizens and their appointed governor. The government was based on the city-state system. This system of government had two assemblies—one, the upper house of "elders"; and the other, the lower house of "men." As outside military pressures were brought to bear on the democratic city-states, the assemblies elected a military head, who finally became a king. Thus began the royal dynasties. Being militarily minded, the kings developed the regular army into formidable forces. They developed the war chariot, drawn by wild asses. The chariots, preceded in warfare by the "artillery" of bows and arrows, were followed by the heavily armored infantry of lancers who attacked in phalanx formation.

The fine development of government was paralleled with a high sense of justice. Codes of law were written as early as the twenty-fourth and twenty-first centuries B.C. Ur-Nammu, king of Ur in 2050 B.C., the time when Terah may have lived in Ur, was noted not only for his military prowess but for his social reforms and laws. He ordered that all "chiselers" and grafters be removed from the land; he established standards for honest weights and measures; he personally saw to it that the orphan, the widow, and the poor man did not fall prey to the wealthy or more powerful. The Code of Ur-Nammu goes beyond the *lex talionis* ("eye for an eye") concept of law. This code orders that fines shall be paid by the guilty party rather than requiring "a tooth for a tooth" or "an eye for an eye" approach! (We wonder if Amos and Isaiah had heard of this great man's prophetic concerns for justice?) In this time great numbers of legal documents were drawn up, including contracts, deeds, promissory notes, wills, court decisions, and receipts.

Supporting the system of law and government was the foundation of religion, as symbolized by the temple, which was the center of social, economic, and political life. Each city-state had its own temple—a *ziggurat* (one of which is referred to as the tower of Babel, Gen. 11:1-9). A ziggurat was a large building, usually made like a stepped pyramid. On the top was a lovely shrine housing the major deity

of the city. The interior walls of the ziggurat were beautifully carved and delicately designed with frescoes of geo-
metric designs, as well as animal and human figures. The
temple was the heart of the city life. The kings of both
Sumer and Akkad, as well as Hammurabi, felt that their
laws were divinely given.[1]

If Terah (and possibly Abraham as a boy) had been
reared near Ur, it is barely possible that Abraham may
have attended school. We are told that Terah was a
wealthy man. As a son of wealth Abraham may have been
given an education. At any rate, the educated of Ur were
trained in reading and writing in cuneiform.[2] Codes of
law (such as those noted above) were studied, teaching the
educated that they had a responsibility toward the orphan,
the widow, and the oppressed poor. Both instrumental and
vocal music were taught. Beautiful harps and lyres have
been excavated from the royal tombs of Ur. Apparently
the people had a kind of orchestra, with harps, lyres, and
double-piped clarinets of both reed and metal.

Though the average student would probably have
studied the legends of his day, it is likely that these were
memorized by youth entering the priesthood. These legends
were considered sacred and holy by the people. They told
of a great flood in the days of a man named Utnapishtim.
They told how he had built an ark (shaped like a cube),
how he had brought animals of all species inside it, and
how it had rained so severely and so long that all mankind
were drowned. After the rains ceased and the waters re-
ceded, Utnapishtim released three birds—a dove, a swallow, and a raven—until he was assured that the earth had
reappeared. Then he offered great sacrifices to his gods.
This story is very similar to, and also quite different from,
the account in Gen. 6–8.

---

[1] The Code of Hammurabi portrays the king receiving the 3,600 lines of
law from Chemosh, the state god of Babylon.

[2] Cuneiform refers to the wedge-shaped characters in the alphabet which
were used in the writing of ancient inscriptions of Assyria, Babylonia, Persia,
and so forth.

Another sacred story of those days had to do with the creation of the world; another, with the fall of man. These deeply impressive stories (known to Sumerians, Akkadians, Hittites, Hurrians, and Amorites) were brought to the land of Canaan and were reworked until eventually they were put in the form in which we find them in Genesis 1–11. Who else would have brought them but those who received the cultural heritage of Sumer and Akkad—including Abraham himself!

But the religion of Sumer, Akkad, and the neo-Sumerian peoples assumed the existence of many gods, each of whom had to be bathed, served his meals, and appeased. Furthermore, religion was a matter of state. The state priests would climb the great stairway (the "ladder" of Jacob's dream) of the ziggurat to the shrine on top in order to worship their moon-goddess, Sin, but the common man could not do so. He was dependent on the small man-made house gods that could be purchased from street hawkers. It is quite possible that here the sensitive Abraham became aware that man-made gods are not truly gods, and that no man can permit another man (a state priest) to do his worshiping for him. Abraham could have had these religious insights in either Ur or Haran, for both cities had ziggurats, and both worshiped the moon-goddess, Sin.

The heart of this faith dealt with fertility. This meant that fertility deities played a great part in the worship. The cult centered around the temple with its priests, priestesses, eunuchs, singers, and musicians. Fertility of flocks and soil were guaranteed to the people by their participation in fertility rites. The rites included sexual relations in the hope that these acts would induce the gods to fertilize the land, flocks, and wives. It was in this setting that Abraham heard the call of God to leave Ur and go to a new country. (We shall leave the discussion of the covenant with God for Part III of this book.)

The family, as in America, was considered the basic unit of society. The members of the family were bound together by love, respect, and mutual obligations. However, the father had absolute authority over his children and was held responsible for their actions. A good father wanted his child to be educated. His training was twofold: intellectual and moral. By the time of Hammurabi (1720 B.C.), boys were studying quadratic equations, logarithms, and elementary astronomy, and were developing grammars and lexicons of several languages. But a "wise" Sumerian (and neo-Sumerian) was noted not only for a quick intellect but also for his moral wisdom. He loved both the good and the true, law and order, justice and freedom, mercy and compassion, justice and loyalty. A wise man hated the liar, the lawless, the unjust, the disorderly, the cruel.

INFLUENCE OF THE AMORITE CULTURE

The time came when Terah and his family migrated to Haran. The decades of the second millennium B.C. were turbulent times. Some "westerners" (called Amorites, a Semitic group) were invading the Mesopotamian world. Many of them came from the desert areas seeking a homeland in the civilized cities. It was a period of civil war and general unrest. Probably it was during these days of Amorite movements that Terah and his family left Ur, passing through the Amorite city-state of Mari till they finally came to an area in northwestern Mesopotamia. It seems likely that they gave the name of Abraham's brother, Haran, to the area—for the city's name is very similar in spelling to that of Abraham's brother. (The only difference in spelling is that in the Hebrew the type of H used is different in the two words.)

Of special interest is the fact that the genealogical list of Abraham's ancestors (in Gen. 11:10 and following) includes names that are also names of cities in the area of Haran. Among these are Haran, Nahor (another of Abraham's brothers), Terah, Sarugdi (Serug), and Phaliga (Peleg). Some scholars think that possibly these were originally partiarchal clan names and were later given by the clans to the towns. These were all Semitic people.

The ancient city of Haran is located on the Balikh River, about sixty miles above the point where the Balikh empties into the Euphrates River.

The Arameans at Haran lived in the land between the two rivers, the Euphrates and Tigris. In fact, Gen. 24:10 refers to it as "Aram-of-the-two-rivers." [3] Haran was also located between two great cities, Carchemish on the west and Nineveh on the east. Great trade routes ran through Haran to these cities.

In the days of King Josiah, and the prophet Jeremiah, Judeans were taught to say: "A wandering Aramean was my father" (Deut. 26:5). Their ancestors had come from "Aram-between-the-two-rivers," in the locality of Haran. It was here at Haran that Terah, father of Abraham, died and that Abraham lived for many years before going to Canaan. At Haran, Jacob married Leah and Rachel. There they gave birth to Jacob's eleven sons (only Benjamin being born outside of Haran). So the patriarchs and their descendants thought of Haran as their ancestral homeland. It is proper to think of the patriarchs as Semitic Arameans.

Since we locate the patriarchal homeland in Haran, we should see their relationship to the Amorite invasion of this area, about 2000 B.C. Actually, the wandering Aramean becomes the invading Amorite.

The Amorites were a truly great people. By the eighteenth century the Amorites had developed a great civilization. The city of Mari, on the Euphrates River (between Haran and Ur), was a magnificent capital. The palace of King Zimri-Lim consisted of nearly three hundred rooms, covering more than fifteen acres. It was a veritable showplace of the world. His archives consisted of over twenty thousand clay tablets—a library that scholars enjoy poring over even today! The documents in the archives contain

---

[3] The Greek word for "between the two rivers" is Mesopotamia. So the land between the two rivers (Tigris and Euphrates) refers to Mesopotamia, which is sometimes also called Naharaim.

two biblical names, Benjamin and David. David, in their literature, means "chieftain," which may well be the meaning as used in our Scripture, too. Mari was finally captured by the great Semitic ruler, Hammurabi, about 1700 B.C. (Some scholars believe that it was during the reign of Hammurabi that Abraham migrated to Canaan.)

THE INFLUENCE OF THE HURRIAN CULTURE

The Hurrians are the biblical Hivites, or Horites (Gen. 36:2, 20). This non-Semitic people lived in the central part of the Mesopotamian world. Thus they were neighbors of the citizens of Nahor, and of Haran. Hurrians also lived in Jerusalem, Shechem, and Syria. Their influence on the patriarchs may well be seen through some of their social customs, as found by archaeologists at Nuzi. Nuzi is southeast of Nineveh on the Tigris River.

One of the most impressive examples of Hurrian influence is seen in Rachel's taking of the teraphim, the family gods (Gen. 31:19, 30). We learn from Nuzi records that a father who had no male heir could adopt his son-in-law as his son. The right to the father's property was guaranteed if the "son" had the teraphim. So we now understand why Rachel took her father's (Laban's) teraphim. She wanted Jacob, her husband, rather than her brother, to inherit the family estate.

Another Hurrian influence is found in the story about Abraham's prayer, "O Lord God, what wilt thou give me, for I continue childless, and the heir of my house is Eliezer of Damascus?" (Gen. 15:2). We now know that the Hurrian custom was for a childless couple to adopt a son (often a person from whom they had borrowed money). This adopted son (their heir) was to take care of them in their old age and see to their burial. But the adoption (and inheritance) was nullified with the birth of a natural son. Such was the case when Isaac was born to Sarah and Abraham.

The Horites (Hurrians) were in Canaan as well as in Mesopotamia when Abraham migrated to the land of promise. He found them at Shechem where he built an altar and offered his first sacrifice in Canaan. Both Isaac and Jacob were in continual neighborly relations with these people. Their influence is seen in many of the Hurrian customs held in common by the Semitic patriarchs and the non-Semitic Hurrians.

Hurrian customs also explain how Esau could sell his birthright to his brother Jacob for a mess of lentils. Nuzi tablets tell about a brother who sold a grove, which he had inherited, to his brother for three sheep. We also learn about deathbed wills, like that of Jacob (Gen. 49) and, more significantly, of Isaac (Gen. 27:33).

The historical background of the various customs of Sumerians, Akkadians, Amorites, and Hurrians helps us see that we are dealing with authentic events which occurred among Israel's various ancestors. We should view the migrations and events of their days against the background of the cultures from which they came and into which they entered—as in the land of Canaan, with its Horites (called Jebusites and Gibeonites in the Old Testament), Amorites, and Canaanites. In this setting Joseph, the beloved son of Jacob, was reared as a boy, sold into slavery by his brothers, and imprisoned in Egypt. We turn now to the historical setting of this patriarch.

The Patriarch Joseph

Joseph, first born of Jacob's favorite wife Rachel, was born in Haran. He was but a boy when his family left Haran to return to Canaan, where Jacob's father Isaac and brother Esau lived. The family settled in Hebron, a dozen miles south of Bethlehem. The biblical account of Jacob's first meeting with his twin brother Esau since the day he had dishonestly received the family blessing and inheritance is interestingly related in Gen. 33. Reconciled, the twin brothers shared in the filial duty of burying their father, Isaac (Gen. 35:29).

A possible dating for Joseph may be made just after the time of the coming of the Hyksos, about 1720 B.C. The Hyksos were a group of "shepherd kings" (mostly of Semitic, Hurrian, and Indo-European stock) who came from the north to Egypt. Num. 13:22 states that Hebron was founded seven years after the founding of Zoan. When the Hyksos built their capital in Egypt, they built it in the Delta, and named it Avaris. Here Joseph ruled the land as governor. Avaris was later called Rameses (in the days of Moses), and finally Zoan (Tanis) after 1100 B.C. We may safely assume that Joseph's boyhood was spent in Hebron at the beginning of the seventeenth century B.C.

When Abraham sojourned in southern Canaan, Hebron had not yet been founded. He dwelt near the Oaks of Mamre—which eventually became the city Hebron. It seems apparent that by the time of Joseph city life had begun to develop. Though Joseph's brothers were still shepherds, we may assume that he and his father, Jacob, were no longer living in tents. That Jacob had given up tent life is suggested by the fact that he had built himself a *house* in Succoth. We note that Joseph stayed behind with his father in Hebron while his brothers cared for the flocks in Shechem. This suggests that they had settled down to one place—thus beginning village life. We also must take into account the implications of "sheaves" in Joseph's dreams—that is, it implies awareness of, if not experience with, farm life. So Jacob's family is only seminomadic by this time (about 1700 B.C.).

The biblical narrative tells how Joseph, the favorite son of Jacob, was sold by his brothers to the Midianites, who in turn apparently sold him in Egypt. Joseph was imprisoned by Potiphar, whose wife used an old and well-known literary motif in Egypt to accuse Joseph of attempted rape. Imprisoned, he showed his ability as a master at interpreting dreams and eventually interpreted the pharaoh's dreams. In recognition of his ability, he was made governor of Egypt.

A Semite, such as Joseph, could have become a chief officer of the court in the days of the Hyksos. The Hyksos ("Rulers of Foreign Countries") were Asiatics who came from the north. These invading Asiatics not only captured Egypt about 1720 B.C., but controlled Egypt for 140 years! It was during their reign over Egypt that we may think of Joseph as governor of Egypt. The Hyksos introduced the horse and chariot to Egypt. The chariot revolutionized warfare and hunting.

Joseph, wearing the golden chain of authority around his neck and a signet ring[4] on his finger, probably rode in a chariot as he inspected the state granaries. It was his task to see that the silos and granaries were filled in preparation for the "lean" years of famine ahead. Egyptian inscriptions tell us of such years of famine, and also tell of how shepherds were permitted to come to the Delta for pasturage during such years of drought.

Archaeological discoveries show that the biblical accounts of Joseph give an accurate description of Egyptian customs, habits, manner of administration by the ruling pharaohs, and of the generosity of these rulers in permitting nomadic peoples to live in their lands during times of drought. These details help us to view Joseph as an historical person in a very real setting. New land reforms were introduced by the Hyksos (possibly by Joseph himself): The land, once owned by nobility, was purchased from them (during the years of drought as in Gen. 47:13-21) by the government. When the Hyksos had been driven from Egypt about 1580 B.C. the land was under the control, not of the nobility, but of a bureaucracy of government officials. So we see Joseph as not only governor but also as originator of a social revolution in Egypt.

---

[4] The signet ring was often a gold ring set with a scarab. The scarab (in the form of a beetle) was incised on the underneath portion with the seal, or name of the owner. The scarab was on a swivel so that the seal could readily be used for sealing a document.

CHAPTER 2

Moses: Prince of Egypt, Deliverer, and Covenant Maker

JOSEPH'S FATHER, Jacob, and his eleven brothers came to Goshen, the eastern portion of the Delta of Egypt, in time of drought. As governor of Egypt, Joseph was able to give them grain and to obtain permission for them to use the land of Goshen for pasturing their sheep.

Scholars have reasons to believe that many decades after Joseph's death, the majority of the tribes ("brothers" of Joseph) returned to Canaan—possibly driven out when the Hyksos were driven from Egypt by the Egyptians, about 1580 B.C. The Semitic brothers of Joseph found grazing lands in the hill country of Canaan—mostly around Shechem, where Abraham had constructed his first altar in Canaan. The remaining "house of Joseph" stayed in Goshen, pasturing their sheep.

The time came, as Exodus tells us, when "there arose a new king over Egypt, who did not know Joseph" (Exod. 1:8). The new king or pharaoh was probably Seti I, who ruled Egypt from 1308 to 1290 B.C. During his reign he apparently was afraid to let these Semitic people remain free in the Delta. They might join forces with some group from Canaan and become a formidable foe in warfare. So Seti I issued a decree ordering that all of these "Apiru" (a foreign group on the edges of Egypt) be put to forced labor. In the records of Ramses II (1290–1224 B.C.) some of these Apiru are represented as dragging stones for his temples. We would probably be correct in identifying these Apiru with the "Hebrews." Seti and Ramses II were both Egyptians, and would not have been interested in anything a Semite such as Joseph had done in the past for their hated Hyksos rulers. Little wonder that the new rulers did not know what Joseph had done. As a matter of fact, the Hebrews did not dare tell about such things!

From this setting of enforced slavery of the Hebrews the story of Israel's greatest hero, Moses, emerges.

Moses, Prince of Egypt

The biblical record tells us that Moses was taken from the waters of the Nile and adopted by a princess of Egypt. Many scholars assume that he was educated as though he were a prince of Egypt. What was Egypt like in the days of Moses' boyhood?

In the first place, it seems likely that he was a youth in the days when Seti I was pharaoh of Egypt. Seti I had a son, Ramses II, who became world renowned. It seems likely that Seti I is the "pharaoh of the oppression" while Ramses II is the pharaoh of the Exodus. It is quite possible that Ramses II and Moses knew each other well as boys. Hieroglyphic inscriptions record that Egyptian pharaohs often trained the sons of nobility whose fathers the pharaoh had captured. It may well be that Moses was educated with such a group. Or he may have been educated according to the standards for sons of Egyptian nobility or royalty.

As a student, Moses would have studied many interesting courses. First, he would have learned to read and write hieroglyphics (picture writing) and demotic (the cursive style of writing). He would have learned elementary geometry and how to draw graphs used to make reproductions from small paintings for the large walls of tombs and other inscriptions. Moses would have been trained in many languages too. Nobility were trained to communicate with peoples of many lands: Nubians, Lybians, Hittites, Philistines (early Greeks), Kenites, Canaanites, Arameans, and Hebrews. They were also trained in the responsibilities of being foremen of an estate, and they were instructed in military strategy.[1]

Besides these significant studies, Moses may have been trained in the social graces befitting a prince of Egypt. He would have been taught to appreciate orchestral music (harps, lyres, flutes, two-pronged metal clarinets, percussion, and so forth), and possibly even to play some of the instruments.

Some scholars believe Moses received some of his education in the priestly schools of On, the same school where Akh-en-Aton studied. This would be a remarkable coincidence, if it were true, because both Akh-en-Aton and Moses believed that there was one God. Akh-en-Aton, who lived during the first half of the fourteenth century (only a few decades before Moses), prayed: "O sole God, greater than whom there is no other, thou hast created the world according to the desires of thy heart." This "first world monotheist" taught that men should *love* God, not fear him. He sometimes began his prayers with the words: "My father who art in heaven . . ." Moses too may have taught that men should *love* the Lord with all their hearts and minds, and that there was but one God: "Hear, O Israel: The LORD our God is one. . . ." (Deut. 6:4). Even so, Moses brought a uniqueness to religion that had never been known in Egypt before—the idea of a covenant relationship with God.

Seti I had started the construction of a beautiful city in the very place where Joseph had been governor four hundred years earlier. It was the Hyksos capital, Avaris, now to be named, not for Seti, as this pharaoh apparently hoped, but "Rameses." It is one of two cities which were store cities, a kind of military depot, for Egypt. The other city is Pithom. Both Rameses and Pithom are mentioned in Exod. 1:11. Pharaoh Seti I and his son Ramses constructed huge statues, temples, and pylons—all of which needed slave

---

[1] Ancient legends tell of Moses' military strategy in wars of Nubia.

labor to do the hard work. Some of the huge statues of Ramses II weighed a thousand tons each, being over forty feet in height and visible for many miles. In moving the Egyptian capital from Thebes (several hundred miles up the Nile from Cairo) to Rameses, the pharaoh planned to make a showplace for the world. And he succeeded! As lovely as Thebes was, the new capital far exceeded it in beauty. Especially beautiful was the temple dedicated to the old Hyksos god Seth, who still remained lord of the city which was founded four hundred years earlier. Many obelisks also beautified the city.

Apparently it was during some work under the direction of Seti I that an Egyptian brutally punished a Hebrew slave. Moses had obviously not lost sight of the fact that the color of his skin and formation of his body were not really Egyptian but Semitic. When he saw the fellow Hebrew abused, he took his part and killed the Egyptian overseer. (Moses was always concerned about the oppressed, though his method of dealing with them was to change during the decades.) The next day he had to face the fact that his act had not been done in solitude but had been seen by others. This meant that his crime of murder of an Egyptian could be reported, and his life would be forfeited. The only possible way out was to flee the land, which he did.

Exodus tells us that Moses fled to Midian, where he spent many years of his life. He married Zipporah, a daughter of Jethro, a "Kenite" (literally, "smith"—meaning a copper-smith), who was a priest of Midian as well as a shepherd. From him Moses learned a great deal about God, whom he soon learned to call "Yahweh" (Exod. 3:15).

Moses, Deliverer from Bondage

Israel has always looked back to the great leader, Moses, as the man through whom God delivered them from slavery in Egypt. Unfortunately, there are no known Egyptian

records that report the events of the Exodus. This does
not mean the Exodus never took place. It probably means
that the events were not considered as significant by Egypt's
rulers as they were by the people of Israel. In this section
we shall not deal with the theological point of view of
the delivery but with the historical and geographical set-
tings in which the man Moses delivered his people from
bondage.

After many attempts by Moses to get the pharaoh's permission to leave Egypt, the time finally came when they
were permitted to go. Their journey apparently was as
follows: In order to leave Goshen, they went south of the
store city Rameses, going directly south for about thirty
miles to Succoth. (Pithom was only a few miles west.)
From here they went eastward to the wilderness of Etham,
then, for reasons unknown, they turned north-westward
again, encamping at Baal-zephon. Baal-zephon is the early
name of the Egyptian town called Tahpanhes where Jeremiah was forced to go after the murder of Gedaliah (Jer.
43:7-9). From this point they had to face the Sea of Reeds
(*Yam Suph*, in Hebrew, is properly translated Reed Sea
rather than Red Sea). This marsh is probably the one at
the southern tip of Lake Menzaleh. This is the likely place
for the eventful crossing of the *Yam Suph*, whose waters
were held back by "a strong east wind all night" (Exod.
14:21).

Having crossed the sea, Israel then faced the desertlike
Sinai, which is about 150 miles wide at the northern part
of the peninsula. Moses, however, had spent forty years in
the area of Mt. Sinai and knew where he was going. He
led them directly south-eastward to Mt. Sinai.

Moses, Covenant Maker

At Mt. Sinai Moses climbed to the heights to be with God.
It seems likely that the training of his Hebrew parents
mingled with that of his Egyptian foster-mother, the

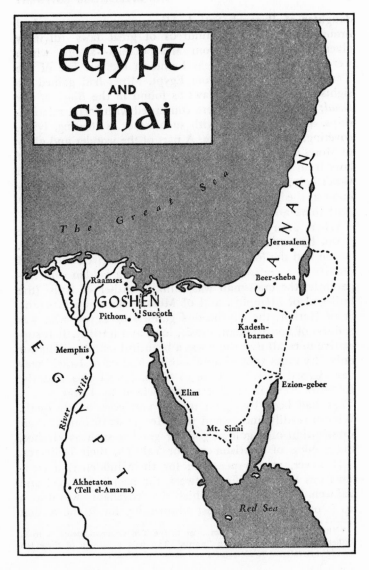

EGYPT **AND** SINAI

The Great Sea

CANAAN

Jerusalem

Raamses

Beer-sheba

GOSHEN

Pithom   Succoth

Kadesh-barnea

E
G
Y
P
T

Memphis

Elim

Ezion-geber

Mt. Sinai

Akhetaton
(Tell el-Amarna)

River Nile

Red Sea

daughter of Pharaoh Seti I. His parental ancestors had
brought memories of hundreds of great laws (divinely
given, they claimed) from Mesopotamia—among which
were the social concerns as found in the last five of the
Ten Commandments. From Egypt, Moses had gained insights from such moral laws as found in the *Book of the
Dead;* laws which also were concerned with social relationships. This book deals with such issues as stealing, lying,
coveting, gossiping, killing. A part of the wonder and glory
of Moses is the fact that, with all this knowledge of scores of
laws from many lands, he was able to reduce them, with
God's help, to ten basic principles, or laws. These we now
know as the Ten Commandments (Exod. 20 and Deut. 5).[1]
And these are still basic for nations in our time.

When, after forty days' absence, Moses returned to the
plain, he was tormented and infuriated by what he saw.
Aaron and the former slaves of Egypt had given their gold
jewelry to a craftsman who made them a golden calf. Apparently, the craftsman was thinking either of Apis (the
bull god of Memphis, and of Mesopotamia and Canaan)
or of Hathor, the cow-headed goddess of Egypt, who was
goddess of nourishment, music, love, and fertility. It is sug-
gestive to recall that there was a beautiful temple of Hathor
only fifty miles west of Sinai—the "children of Israel" may
have passed by it en route to Sinai. Recall also that the
Israelites were in a desert area where food was scarce.
They had been living on manna and occasionally quail.
We can readily understand why Moses was furious at their
substitution of a golden god, or goddess such as Hathor,
the goddess of nourishment, for Yahweh, their Deliverer.

However, after repentance for their infidelity, a covenant was finally ratified between the people of Israel and
Yahweh. The manner in which the "covenant" was drawn
up is of very great interest historically, for it shows that

---

[1] The Old Testament does not refer to the Ten Commandments as such.
Rather, they are called the ten "words." The later expansion of these ten
"words" are referred to as statutes and commandments.

Moses knew the very latest method of drawing up a treaty
between a great ruler and a people. In the second millennium B.C., there were two kinds of treaties; the *parity*
treaty (made between those who considered themselves
equal), and the *suzerainty* treaty (made between a great
king and his vassal or subjects). Our interest is in the
suzerainty treaties which the Hittites were using in the fourteenth and fifteenth centuries B.C.

An analysis of the Hittite suzerainty treaties shows the
following basic elements:

The preamble. The treaty begins with an identification
of the sovereign: "These are the words of . . . (then the
name of the king appears), the Great King . . . (his titles),"
and so forth.

The historical prologue. Here is described the acts of
benevolence which the suzerain has performed in behalf
of his vassal. The vassal is to respond to these mercies by
gratitude, and thus show willingness to accept the suzerain's
obligations.

The stipulations. Here the sovereign stipulates the obligations he requires of the vassal if he would bind himself in covenant with him. One of the requirements is
military: He must not enter into alliances with other independent kings; he must always be an enemy of the king's
enemies and a friend of his friends. The vassal is under
obligation to answer any of the sovereign's summons for
military forces. The vassal is required to divide the booty
of war with his sovereign, according to the sovereign's
will. There is to be no "murmuring" against the sovereign
—the vassal is to trust him.

The deposit and public reading. The treaty is to be deposited in the sanctuary of the vassal and to be read in public at regular intervals—from one to four times a year.

The list of witnesses. The gods of both states—those of
the vassal and those of the sovereign—are named, and also
such witnesses as the mountains, rivers, sea, heaven, and
earth, winds, and so forth. A breach of contract will be

punished by the gods; hence, an appeal to awe is made as the covenant is ratified.

The blessings and curses. They are to be disbursed by the divine witnesses according to whether the covenant was maintained or broken.

The oath. This, if given, was taken by the vassal and was apparently a solemn ritual. We are uncertain as to its content since none of the oaths were written in the treaty.

If one of the parties died, the covenant was no longer binding. Hence, the great number of "rebellions" at the death of a sovereign king. Likewise, when a vassal died, his successor was required to renew the covenant with the sovereign king by taking the oath. There is no known covenant held in perpetuity—which suggests the wisdom of the requirement that each vassal and each generation renew their covenant themselves, thus producing a relevance of the covenant for each generation.

Scholars have pointed out that the Mosaic covenant was very similar to the suzerainty treaties, which is not surprising to us since Moses, educated in Egypt, would probably have been familiar with the treaties which Seti I had made with the Hittites in his lifetime.

Let us note a few similarities, especially in Exod. 20 and Josh. 24 (see also Deut. 5), which are good illustrations of the Mosaic covenant:

THE HITTITE SUZERAINTY TREATY	THE MOSAIC DECALOGUE
1. The Preamble: The acts of the sovereign's benevo-Great King . . ."	"Thus says the LORD, the God of Israel" (Josh. 24:2). "I am the LORD" (Exod. 20:1).
2. The Historical Prologue: The acts of the sovereign's benevolences are listed.	"I . . . brought you out of the land of Egypt, out of the house of bondage" (Exod. 20:2). Josh. 24:2-13 adds that the Lord gave them the promised land in which to dwell.

3. The Stipulations:
The sovereign agrees to provide for and to protect his subjects, while the subjects agree not to seek security in relations with any other foreign powers.

"You shall have no other gods before me" (Exod. 20:3).
"Put away the gods which your fathers served beyond the River (that is, at Haran on the Euphrates River) and in Egypt, and serve the LORD" (Josh. 24:14).

4. The Deposit and Public Reading:
The sovereign requires the treaty to be deposited in the sanctuary of the vassal, and to be read in public at regular intervals.

(Josh. 24:26) and Deut. (31:9-12) require that the covenant be placed in charge of the priests, who carried the Ark of the Covenant. They are instructed to read the agreement (covenant) at the end of every seventh year.

5. List of Witnesses:
The gods and other witnesses are to keep an eye on the covenant makers in order to punish any breach of contract.

"You are witnesses" (Josh. 24:22). If they break the covenant; they will witness against themselves! This is a new idea in covenant making. Note that witnesses of earth and sky, mountains, and rivers were still used by Israel, as seen in the prophets (Isa. 1:2 and Mic. 6:1-2).

6. The Blessings and Curses:
These are to be disbursed by the divine witnesses.

"If you forsake the Lord and serve foreign gods, then he will turn and do you harm, and consume you, after having done you good" (Josh. 24:20).

7. The Oath:
A solemn ritual.

"And the people said to Joshua, 'The Lord our God we will serve, and his voice we will obey.' So Joshua made a covenant with the people that day" (Josh. 24: 24-25).

The covenant established through the work of Moses suggests not only his keen knowledge of treaties but also his fine ability to transfer such knowledge to the realm of religion—to man's relationship to God. Moses laid the base for believing that loyalty and obedience are man's obligations to a God who loved, saved, and provided for him. We shall see in Part III how this interpretation of God's activity in her history became the ground for the faith of Israel. The point we desire to emphasize here is the use Moses made of the forms of the suzerainty treaties of his day. We understand the style, and perhaps even the content, of the ten "words" better as we learn of the historical background out of which the covenant came.

From Slavery to a Fighting Force

After Moses had guided his people in their acceptance of the covenant with Yahweh, he sent spies to Canaan, the promised land, to consider the possibilities of capturing the land through immediate warfare. The spies, with the exception of two men, Joshua and Caleb, returned with negative reports. They saw the great walled cities of Canaan —cities whose walls sometimes were fifty feet high and thirty feet thick. Some cities had two walls! They recognized the safety which the towers on the city walls gave to their inhabitants; they observed the added strength of military chariots—their mobility and power. The Israelites had no chariots. They also saw that the land was "a land of milk and honey." But the report was governed by their fear of the military might and security of the Canaanites. So it was that Moses was forced to wait an entire generation, until the former slaves were replaced through death by fearless young men, before he could lead them toward the land promised to Abraham (Gen. 12:1-3).

During these years of waiting Moses acted as judge and religious leader of his people. They lived in the area of Kadesh-barnea, in the desert areas south of Beersheba.

There is an oasis at Kadesh-barnea which would easily take care of several thousand persons. It will be remembered that very likely most of Joseph's relatives who came to Egypt during the Hyksos period had returned to Canaan. This large group of Hebrews had by the time of Moses settled in the area of Shechem, in the hill country of Canaan. The "house of Joseph" is the name given to the Hebrew slaves who had come from Egypt, covenanted with God at Sinai, and were being forged into a tough militant group of people at Kadesh-barnea. We should not think in terms of millions of people at this oasis, but of perhaps five or six thousand persons. A generation later they will be joined by their blood-relatives as they fight for a homeland and form a confederacy at Shechem (Josh. 24), but the core of Israel is this smaller group who were forged by Moses at Kadesh-barnea into a deeply religious people, a people who acknowledged the special providence of Yahweh.

At the close of the generation Moses led his people toward Edom. Being refused the right to cross its borders, he led them around that country, first southward and then eastward, until they could go northward toward Moab. With little apparent difficulty these militant descendants of slaves won a ready victory over Moab. From Mt. Nebo, one of the sacred hills of Moab, Moses viewed the "promised land" and placed the mantle of leadership on a young man named Hoshea. Shortly after Moses renamed Hoshea "Joshua" ("Yahweh will save"), Moses died on the hills of the newly conquered Moab. Joshua assumed command, and the stage was set for the conquest of Canaan.

CHAPTER 3

The Conquest of Canaan—
Period of the Judges—Monarchy

When Joshua, Moses' successor, stood on Mt. Nebo, and contemplated how his army would take Canaan, he little realized what interesting people lived in Canaan. Canaan was a melting pot of the world—people from many nations had migrated to this small country, a land no larger than the state of New Hampshire. We have already noted some of the people who lived here. There were Amorites and Arameans (from whom the patriarchs came), and Horites (Hurrians, many of whose customs were adopted by the patriarchs). Besides these, there were Hittites, who had had a great kingdom in Mesopotamia in the second millennium B.C. Some of them had migrated to Canaan, especially around Hebron. Then, too, there were the Semitic Canaanites, with their exceedingly fine culture.

The Canaanites lived for the most part in the lowlands. Their cities were surrounded by one or two walls, which sometimes were as high as fifty feet. They had a city-state form of government with a king as their head. During the period when Joshua invaded their land, these city-states of Canaan were under the authority of Egypt, whose tax collectors were noted for their harshness and greediness. Each city-state had its king (and his palace) and nobility; the feudal system governed the life of the common man, who was subject to forced labor, taxation, and military service of his king. The Canaanite military forces employed war chariots to great advantage. (Their use of the chariot explains in part why they did not live in the mountains, where chariots could not be used.) Archaeologists have found beautiful delicately carved ivory inlays of all kinds, gold and copper jewelry and vessels, and bronze instruments for agriculture and war. Some of the strongly fortified Canaanite cities which the Israelites could not conquer included a chain of cities in the north (Dor, Megiddo, Ibleam, Taanach, Bethshan), and in the south (Gezer and Jerusalem).

Within four decades after Joshua entered Canaan, he had to face the might of a new and powerful enemy, the Philistines. These people brought the iron age to Palestine shortly after 1192 B.C. They came from Asia Minor and possibly from the island of Crete where their ancestors had known the remarkable Minoan and Mycenaean civilizations. The Philistines held the pentapolis, five cities on the southern coast of Palestine: Ashkelon, Ashdod, Gaza, Ekron, and Gath. They, or "near relatives," conquered the Canaanite city of Dor, a city south of Mt. Carmel, and later occupied Bethshan and the plain of Esdraelon.

Joshua had been one of the two spies (the other was Caleb) who had recommended to Moses a generation earlier at Kadesh-barnea that the Hebrews invade Canaan. He had seen their fine city fortifications, their military methods of warfare (including the chariot), and must have known of the many types of people who lived in Canaan. Now, as he faced the crossing of the Jordan, he felt ready to attack these cities. He and Moses had successfully conquered the Moabites and the kingdoms of Sihon and Og, and had given the land to Reuben, the half-tribe of Manasseh, and Gad. (Edom, Moab, Sihon, Og, and Ammon were all newly founded countries in thirteenth century B.C.) With his forces having tasted victory in warfare, Joshua was ready to go into Canaan. The spades of archaeologists attest that the time of his fiery invasion must have been around 1225 B.C.

The Conquest of Canaan

The book of Joshua states that there were three major thrusts against Canaan—in the central, southern, and northern areas of Canaan. The book of Judges states that the land was not wholly conquered under Joshua, but that it took a long time (two hundred years) for Israel to capture the land. Both views may be harmonized when we realize that Joshua, while unable to capture all the cities of Canaan, did "break the back" of the city-state system of Canaan, thus leaving the "mopping up" task to military forces of kings who came after him, especially the armies of Saul and David.

Having crossed the Jordan River, Joshua led in the capture of central Canaan. This capture of central Canaan is symbolized (for the land was not completely taken) by the capture of Jericho and Bethel. Jericho in Joshua's day was over seven thousand years old. It had been destroyed innumerable times in the past—more than sixteen city walls had crumbled before this time! By the time Joshua came to Jericho, it was no longer the great city it had been in the days of Abraham. It was not much more than a small fort, and apparently readily fell to Joshua's forces. Having destroyed Jericho, he then led his forces to Bethel. In the biblical account Ai is probably confused with the city of Bethel. Archaeologists have found that Ai was not inhabited from 2400 to 1000 B.C. So Bethel (not Ai) was captured and burned by Joshua and his forces about 1225 B.C. The conflagration was so great in this great city (Bethel) that in some places the ashes of its ruins are five feet deep. With the capture of Jericho and Bethel, the nomadic Hebrews occupied the hill country of central Canaan. At this time, the central mountain ridge was for the most part a wooded land though grazing areas had been cleared for cattle, sheep, and goats.

The second thrust in the capture of Canaan was in the south. Archaeologists have excavated Lachish and found that it was a typically well-walled Canaanite city. It fell to Joshua's forces about 1220 B.C. Then Israel laid seige to Eglon, fought and captured it. Finally they took Hebron, which was easily captured, then laid seige to Debir (Kiriath-sepher) . The conflagration of Debir was so great that three-foot thick layers of ashes still remain as witness of Joshua's destruction of the entire city. The Israelites built a city on the ashes, as was done in Lachish and Bethel.

3 The third thrust in the conquest of Canaan was in the north. The Israelites were apparently unsuccessful in their attempts to take the Canaanite east-west chain of cities in the north—Dor, Megiddo, Ibleam, Taanach, and Bethshan, nor the former granary of Egypt, the plain of Esdraelon. However, the forces did move up beyond the Sea of Galilee to the city of Hazor, a city covering two hundred acres. In Joshua's time, forty thousand people lived there. Since the days of the Hyksos (1720–1580 B.C.) it had been a showplace. Hazor had a corral for horses, with a fifty-foot wall enclosing an area three thousand by two thousand feet. The Hyksos, who first built Hazor, were the ones who brought the horse and chariot to Canaan and Egypt. Solomon later made great use of the horses and chariots in his commercial enterprises. Hazor was also noted for its excellent Canaanite temple, which was similar in many respects to Solomon's temple in Jerusalem.

Josh. 10:31-43 and 11:10-15 refer to the cities mentioned above which archaeologists have excavated. Archaeological discoveries tell us that these cities were completely destroyed in fierce warfare about 1225-1220 B.C., at the very time Joshua was fighting for a homeland in Canaan. We draw the inevitable conclusion: Joshua was the leader of the forces who destroyed these cities which archaeologists have described and their descriptions supplement the accounts in Josh. 10–11.

Historically, one of the most significant events in the life of Israel was the great meeting at Shechem of all the descendants of Jacob. There were two major groups which joined the confederacy at this time at Shechem. First and primary was the invading house of Joseph, under the leadership of Joshua. This group represented those who had gone into Egypt in the time of Joseph, and had remained there. It was their fathers (for the most part the descendants of Benjamin and Joseph—the sons of Jacob and Rachel) who had experienced the years of oppression under Pharaoh Seti I and Ramses II. They were the group perhaps numbering as many as six thousand who had grown up under the agreements of the covenant in the desert of Kadesh-barnea. The second group (for the most part the sons of Jacob and Leah) represents those who had either stayed in Canaan (instead of going to Egypt at the time of Joseph) or had returned when the Hyksos were expelled from Egypt in 1580 B.C. These two groups (the Rachel and Leah tribes) gathered in the hill country at Shechem, between the two mountains, Ebal and Gerizim.

At Shechem, Joshua formed a confederacy based on the covenant concept (see Josh. 24). The union of these two groups at Shechem, where Abraham had first set up an altar in Canaan, marked the point at which the nation was really born. Many scholars believe it received its name "Israel" at this great meeting, the ratification of the covenant by all the tribes at Shechem. The descendants of Jacob were now bound together not by political but by a religious bond. (Recall that this does not include *all* the descendants of Abraham—for some of his descendants included the Ishmaelites, the Arabs, and his "nephews," the Moabites and Ammonites.)

The Nature of the Judges

The period of the judges is roughly 1225-1030 B.C. The "judges" should not be thought of as men of the legal profession. Only Deborah, a woman, seems to have "held court" to adjudicate cases. Furthermore, a person who "judged" Israel in those days was not a national but a tribal leader. He is described as a savior of his tribe (or tribes) in time of trouble.

Each person who "judged" Israel was considered a "charismatic" leader—he had a special gift from God whereby he was set apart from others. The judges should not be thought of as successors to one another, nor as ruling over all the tribes at any one time. The Scriptures refer to only twelve judges, one from each of the twelve "tribes," or divisions of Canaan. Each saved his people, or groups of people, from some foreign invader. Some of the major "judges" were: Othniel, who expelled the Aramaeans in Transjordan; Deborah and Barak, who defeated the Canaanites in the north; Gideon, who repelled the Midianite raiders who attacked central Canaan and the plain of Esdraelon; Jephthah, who defeated the Ammonites; Ehud, who "saved" Israel from the Moabites; Samson, who defeated hundreds of Philistines in the west. This list suggests that a geographical scheme was used by the writer of the book of Joshua—he chose typical persons from various geographical sections of the tribes, and showed how they had saved their people during this period.

Gideon's counterattack on the Midianites was a very dangerous one because the Midianites had introduced something new in warfare—the camel! This incident in the eleventh century B.C. is the first time in history that an invasion was made on camelback. From this time on we note the great use of camels, which were apparently domesticated during this period of history for the first time. Previously men had used asses as beasts of burden. Now, men could travel greater distances across the desert because of the ability of the camel to go long periods of time without water. From this date camel caravans begin to trek across the desert wastes of Arabia.

We should keep in mind that Joshua's forces did not capture all of Canaan at this time. They took several of the major cities but could not conquer them all. So they simply settled down near them. Before long they were fight-

ing common enemies. It is a significant fact that except for
Deborah and Barak, who fought at the plain of Esdraelon
against Sisera, the Canaanites and Israelites fought the same
enemies! Both fought often together against the Moabites,
Midianites, Philistines, Ammonites, and Amorites. Since
they fought side by side, soon they were friends, and finally
many intermarried. Thus, two hundred years after the
time of Joshua, Canaan was assimilated into the Israelite
family tree. But this was not without serious consequences,
for the people of Israel adopted many Canaanite religious
concepts, rituals, and festivals.

We should not overlook the significance of the fact that
both Israelites and Canaanites were Semitic people. They
spoke practically the same language. The name for God
—El—was held in common. The patriarchs used the word
El for God. For example, Jacob called him El-Shaddai.
By 1400 B.C. the Canaanites had developed a very high type
of poetic structure for their religious liturgy and literature.
They were the first to use what we call parallelism. In
Hebrew poetry there is usually a two-line structure, with
the second line (sentence) repeating the first line with
different words, or slightly changing the thought by adding
a new idea, or possibly giving the opposite. The Hebrews,
both prophets and psalmists, borrowed this device from the
Canaanite poets.

When nomadic Israel came into the land of Canaan, the
Canaanites were an agricultural people. They believed that
the land belonged to Baal. Unless he was given a tithe
and offered the first fruits of the land, Baal (the "Lord" of
the land) would not give them rain and fertility the next
year. So the Hebrews, who worshiped Yahweh as the moral
God of Sinai, also learned to worship Baal and his wife
Asherah (Astarte), the god and goddess of fertility. From
the Canaanites the Hebrews learned to make agricultural
offerings: first fruits of the land, and offerings for the feast
of the harvest (thanksgiving) and feast of ingathering.
The worship of the mother goddess, Astarte, who was the

goddess of fertility, included the imitative act of sexual intercourse, which "assured" fertility. The lewdness and sensuality of this act in the name of worship was condemned by the prophets, beginning with Elijah. Elijah ("Yahweh is my God") taught that Yahweh was also the God of fertility; Israel should worship either Yahweh or Baal, but not both! The sensuality of the fertility worship proved to be a troublesome matter for Israel from the days of the judges down to the time of the exile, 586 B.C., and even beyond that date.

Toward the close of the period of the judges anarchy was rampant. The various tribes were not duty bound to fight for one another; no authority could force a common front against the Philistine menace; moral life was becoming degraded (witness the sad social conditions as described in Judg. 19–21); Israel was fast beginning to lose her religious and political unity. The last verse of the book of Judges rightly describes the scene: "In those days there was no king in Israel; every man did what was right in his own eyes" (Judg. 21:25).

The Rise of the Monarchy

By 1050 B.C. the Philistines [1] had practically taken over the hill country of Canaan—the Israelites were being conquered! In fact, some Hebrews were serving in the Philistine army (I Sam. 14:21). The Philistine "know-how" of smelting iron had given them the edge over all other groups. They not only had iron swords, spears, and shields, but they had iron hoes, sickles, mattocks, plowpoints, and pruning hooks. They brought an industrial revolution to Canaan.

Iron does not appear among the artifacts in Israel until the time of Israel's first king, Saul (1020-1000 B.C.). An

---

[1] The Philistines were the motley group of people whose ancestors grew up in Crete, with its great Minoan and Mycenean civilization. These people were the forefathers of the Greeks.

iron plowpoint was found at his fortress-palace at Gibeah. This marks the beginning of the iron age for Israel. It also points up the conflict between Israel and the Philistines. Israel had suffered defeat at the hands of the Philistines when they had captured the ark of the covenant at Aphek and then destroyed the sacred Israelite shrine at Shiloh. These defeats pointed up the need for strong leadership and thorough organization. The Israelites determined to have a king. Samuel, a circuit judge, who had formerly been a servant at the shrine at Shiloh while Eli was priest there, anointed Saul, a Benjaminite, as Israel's first king. He did so at the demands of the people: "We will have a king over us, that we also may be like all the nations" (I Sam. 8:19-20). There can be little doubt but what Samuel considered this a good move (I Sam. 9:1–10:16; 11:1-15).[2]

Saul's time of leadership came when the people of Jabesh-gilead were in great need of military help. Saul sent out a message for all the tribes to report for military duties. He got a ready response and soon routed the Ammonites, who otherwise would have blinded the men of Jabesh-gilead (I Sam. 11:1-11). Saul was popular at once, was hailed as king, and was soon crowned king at Gilgal, where Joshua had set up his first campaign headquarters near the Jordan. Saul's next move was to seek freedom from the Philistine yoke. Through Jonathan's bravery Saul routed the Philistines and cleared the hill country of the Philistines, freeing it again for Israel (I Sam. 13:1–14:46). This was Saul's major contribution.

Saul's capital at Gibeah was small, his palace but a small fortress. He did not initiate taxation or establish a new form of government. Saul was more a chieftain than a king. Yet, by the time of his death, the Philistines had been forced back to the plains of Philistia, the Canaanite strongholds were reduced to only two, Gezer and Jerusalem, and

---

[2] A second view of the monarchy is described in I Sam. 7:15–8:22; 10:17-24; 12. This later view represents a strong criticism of the monarchy, possibly after the monarchy had proved to be despotic and apostate.

a new sense of unity had developed among the Israelites. Saul's downfall came in part when he alienated Samuel, the maker of kings. Samuel told Saul that he would not establish a dynasty and that he (Samuel) had anointed David as the next king, which fact caused Saul considerable melancholia and apparently madness. It was left to David to establish the monarchy in the true sense of the word.

David, the Real Creator of the Monarchy

It seems likely that David was introduced to King Saul as a musician. He apparently played the lyre (rather than the harp), and became known as the sweet singer of Israel. His skill with the sling is well known from the biblical stories of his shepherd life and his killing of the iron-bedecked Philistine, Goliath, in the valley of Elah. He was made a captain of Saul's military forces and proved to be a successful military man.

Jealousy on Saul's part caused a rupture which eventually forced David to become a kind of outlaw. He drew within his circle "every one who was in distress, and every one who was in debt, and every one who was discontented . . . and he became captain over them" (I Sam. 22:2). The group was four hundred strong, later enlarged to six hundred men. They lived in various hideouts in Judah, mostly around Engedi. Finally, David attached himself and his forces to the Philistine king, Achish of Gath. Saul, meanwhile, sought his life.

After Saul's death David was anointed king of Judah at Hebron. At the conclusion of seven and a half years of civil war between Israel and Judah, David was crowned king of Israel as well as Judah. He conquered Jerusalem and made it his political and religious center. He conquered the Philistines, whom Saul had pushed to the sea. He probably had learned their secrets concerning the smelting of iron while serving Achish of Gath. "David prepared iron in abundance for the nails for the doors of the gates, and for the joinings" (I Chron. 22:3 KJV). His building enterprises included a truly royal palace made of cedars from Lebanon, royal government buildings and palaces for his queens.

David established his monarchy with the support of an official staff. He appointed a cabinet which included the chief of the military staff; a commander of his personal army of six hundred; the chief priests; a state recorder, who regulated the ceremonies in the palace, prepared David's itinerary, and acted as public relations man; a scribe, probably an Egyptian, who directed the work of state correspondence; a chief of his legion of honor, "the thirty"; and a court historian. The court historian is the first real historian in history. The biographical writings in II Sam. 9–20, and I Kings 1–2 are considered to be the first recorded history—five centuries before Herodotus of Greece. He may well have written down the oral traditions about the patriarchs as well as an account of God's providential care of Israel, her redemption from Egypt, and the conquest of Canaan. If so, he could be the writer of the "J-document," the southern (Judean) account of the historical life of Israel.[3]

Fortunately for Israel, both Egyptian and Mesopotamian powers were quiescent at this time. Having internal troubles of their own, they left the new monarchy alone. So David took advantage of his times.

He extended the boundaries of Israel on all sides. He won the lands on both sides of the Jordan, and from Mt. Lebanon to the borders of Egypt. Moab, Ammon, Edom, Syria, Philistia, and many Canaanite cities were all subjected to his government and paid taxes to his coffers. From these foreign states came subjects who served him faithfully: Ittai of Gath, a Philistine; Zelek, an Ammonite; Uriah the Hittite; Ithmah, the Moabite; and others. David had unusual powers of drawing loyalty to himself. However, he was unable to command absolute loyalty within his own

---

[3] See pages 82-89 for a discussion of the J-document.

household, as harem intrigues indicate. The stories of Absalom's rebellion, of Adonijah's attempt to become king instead of Solomon, and of Amnon's crime against his half-sister Tamar suggest David's inability to rule his own household. Nonetheless, David's rule became idealized in the minds of later centuries, until the Hebrews looked back to his rule as the Golden Age of Israel.

Solomon, Last Monarch of All Israel

Just prior to his death, David appointed Solomon his royal successor and heir to the throne. This personal appointment was necessary inasmuch as Adonijah was being crowned king at the very same time by another group.

Solomon continued many of David's policies, especially the structure of his official cabinet. He increased taxation and initiated conscription of men into his labor battalions. This manpower was needed because of his great building enterprises: His capital, Jerusalem, was enlarged with new palaces and a beautiful Temple designed by Phoenician artists. He established a string of chariot cities in both north and south, for purposes of collecting taxes from all caravans crossing his borders, and for commerce, selling horses obtained from the north to Egypt, and selling chariots from Egypt to northern peoples. He established a navy in the Gulf of Aqabah, copper mines in the Arabah, and foundries for smelting copper at Ezion-geber. But forced labor was despised by his subjects and became one of the major causes for the disruption of the monarchy at the time of his death.

Solomon was noted also for his scores of treaties with almost all the nations of his day. His method of securing his nation against military attack was to marry the daughter of the king of every nation, thus assuring himself that his father-in-law would not attack him. These treaty alliances with foreign nations via marriage of each king's daughter proved to be of great commercial and cultural advantage too. But one can imagine the anger of those loyal to the Mosaic covenant as they learned of Solomon's marriage to an Egyptian princess! Furthermore, he built her a special palace which called for more money and more manpower.

The cost of supporting this multitude was stupendous. The food consumed in just a day consisted of 337½ bushels of flour, 675 bushels of meal, 10 fattened cattle, 20 pasture-fed cattle, 100 sheep, and many fowl and wild animals, such as gazelle (I Kings 4:22-23). To obtain this supply of food for the court, Solomon divided the kingdom into twelve districts. He appointed a district city and a governor for each district. For example, Megiddo was the governor's city of the fifth district. Great granaries were found by archaeologists in such district cities as Megiddo, Lachish, and Beth-shemesh. These cities had beautiful palaces, paved streets, huge city walls, and excellent paved stables for horses and chariots. Megiddo's stables could care for 450 horses, chariots, and lackeys.

The demands of higher taxation, conscription of men for labor, the high cost of maintaining Solomon's ever-growing harem and court personnel, and religious apostasy encouraged the prophet Ahijah to plot against continuing the Davidic dynasty. Jeroboam, an overseer of the hated labor gangs, was anointed the new king of Israel (of the ten northern tribes) by Ahijah the prophet. With Solomon's death the monarchy was rent in twain. Jeroboam became king of Israel (the ten northern tribes), and Rehoboam, king of Judah.[4]

---

[4] Solomon had divided the land into twelve administrative divisions with a governor over each district. After Solomon's death the monarchy was divided into two independent nations, Israel (which included ten of the administrative divisions, or "tribes"), and Judah (receiving only two of the divisions).

CHAPTER 4

The Two Kingdoms
and Their Downfall

ONE OF THE TRULY great moments of history was the dramatic meeting of the elders of Israel with Rehoboam, son of King Solomon, about 922 B.C. (I Kings 11:43–12:24). The elders of the north, representing the ten "tribes" or Solomon's administrative districts, met at Shechem, before crowning Rehoboam, Solomon's son, as their king. But their concept of kingship required that the king be the servant, not master, of the people. They, therefore, asked the young man, Rehoboam, what his policies would be. His answer, reflecting that of the young men of his social circles rather than the sage counsel of his elders, was that he would lay a heavier yoke upon their backs than his father had done. The northerners immediately repudiated this concept of kingship and refused to accept David's grandson, Rehoboam, as their king.

Jeroboam, who had been in charge of Solomon's labor gangs and who had fled to Egypt because of his own conspiracies for the crown, returned in time to be crowned king of Israel. One of the first things he did was to establish two new religious centers, realizing that pilgrimages to Jerusalem would be harmful to political loyalties. So he had two sanctuaries constructed, one in the south at Bethel and one in the north at Dan. He had craftsmen make two golden bulls and had them installed in the sanctuaries. Archaeologists have found several artifacts which portray the gods of Semitic people as riding on the backs of various animals. Hadad, the storm god of the Canaanites, is shown riding on the back of a bull. Possibly when Jeroboam offered sacrifices (I Kings 12:32), he conceived of the invisible Yahweh as riding on the back of the bull, even as Solomon before him had constructed cherubim over the ark of the covenant as the residence of God. This conception would make the bulls of Dan and Bethel a type of pedestal, above which the invisible Yahweh resided.

The Kingdom of Israel

The kingdom of Israel lasted two centuries. It was filled with court intrigue, murder, assassination, immorality of all kinds, and religious apostasy. Only for brief periods, under Omri and Jeroboam II, did good times come to Israel, and those days lasted only during their reigns. Anarchy and murder of kings was the order of the day.

After Jeroboam's death, about 911 B.C., his son Nadab ruled—but for only a year, then being assassinated by Baasha, who assumed the crown. After Baasha's son, Elah, assumed the crown, he was murdered by Zimri, a general. Zimri took the crown but ruled for only one week before he committed suicide. Omri, a general of the army, succeeded Zimri. He was a strong leader. He built the northern capital at Samaria, which was a lavish affair, as the ivory inlays of Samaria indicate. He is also remembered for the state marriage of his son Ahab to the Phoenician king's daughter, Jezebel. Ahab inherited a strong military force from his father.[1] In the famous battle of Karkar (854 B.C.) Ahab contributed to the coalition of twelve Syrian states two thousand chariots and ten thousand foot soldiers—no small contribution! Ahab is remembered mostly however, for his encounter with the prophets Micaiah (I Kings 22) and

---

[1] Ahab was probably the greatest king Israel, the northern kingdom, ever had. However, the test of a king's greatness for the Deuteronomic writers was not political, but theological—that is, did the king follow in the sins of Jeroboam? Ahab did. The biblical writers do not extol his secular virtues.

Elijah, whom Ahab called the "troubler of Israel" (I Kings 18:17).

We misunderstand Jezebel unless we view her against the background of her religion. Her father, Ethbaal, was priest-king of Tyre, Phoenicia. He worshiped Baal-Melqart, a fertility deity. Jezebel, loyal to her father's faith, attempted to bring her religion to the land to which she came as queen. Not only was she deeply loyal to her religious faith, but she was also accustomed to having her every wish granted because of her royal status. But this was not the custom, even for kings, in Israel.

All Israel, as in Judah, knew that even kings were subject to the moral law and ancient social customs of Israel. In the story of Naboth's vineyard, Elijah affirms the religious responsibility of Naboth not to sell the land, for the land belonged to the Lord. A Hebrew family was a steward of God's land and was held responsible for its care. Naboth was not a landlord; he did not own the land, hence he could not sell it to Ahab. So the conflict between Elijah and Jezebel was not only religious but also moral: It was concerned with the responsibilities for stewardship by the common people. Elijah stood for faith and loyalty to stewardship. Jezebel's policies, resisted by the prophets, started a bloody revolution which caused the destruction of Omri's dynasty within forty years. Jehu, anointed king by Elisha while on the battlefield, began his rule by murdering both King Joram of Israel and King Ahaziah of Judah. Jehu's reign was a bloody one. Later the Assyrian Shalmaneser III portrayed Jehu (on Shalmaneser's obelisk) as his vassal.

The northern kingdom lost all its power and prestige under Jehu's reign. For example, thirty years after the death of the eminently successful king, Ahab, whose contributions to a coalition of states fighting the Assyrians at Karkar had been ten thousand chariots, King Jehu's son could barely muster fifty horsemen and ten chariots. Israel, the northern kingdom, was militarily and politically bankrupt. Eventually Israel recovered some of her lost prestige during the

reign of Jeroboam II (784-744 B.C.) who reconquered the
lands which had been lost after Jehu's ignominious rule.
Great prosperity was recovered during this period. In these
days the voices of Amos and Hosea were heard at Bethel,
speaking against the cruelty of the wealthy who had no
compassion for the widow, the orphan, and the poor man,
and speaking against commitments to gods other than Yahweh. Amos could foresee that nationalistic pride and arrogance mixed with false religion would bring disaster to
Israel.

With Jeroboam's death, anarchy set in again in Israel.
We have noted above how king after king was assassinated.
So again in this period inordinate desires for power and
status brought the assassin's knife to royalty: Zechariah, son
of Jeroboam II, ruled only six months before being
murdered by Shallum, who ruled but one month (744 B.C.)
before being murdered by Menahem. Menahem was succeeded by his son Pekahiah, who was assassinated by Pekah.
Pekah's successor, Hoshea, ruled ten years before the Assyrian forces sent him as a prisoner to Assyria and then
completely devastated the northern kingdom of Israel.

We might summarize the fate of Israel, the northern
kingdom, by noting that the last twenty years of her life
were ones of anarchy and bloodshed: Four of the six kings
who reigned after Jeroboam II were assassinated, one was
captured and died in a prison in Assyria, and only one died
a nonviolent death! (Read Hos. 4 in the light of all this
moral decadance and anarchy.)

The kingdom of Israel was ravaged by Tiglath-pileser III,
the Assyrian, who died in 727 B.C. With his death King
Hoshea, the last king of Israel, rebelled against Assyria,
hoping that Egypt would prove to be a strong source of
security, but it was a groundless hope. Shalmaneser V (successor to Tiglath-pileser), imprisoned Hoshea for rebellion
and besieged Israel for three years.

The city fell in 721 B.C. to Sargon II, successor to Shalmaneser, who had died a month earlier. Sargon, on his

victorious return from Egypt to Assyria, took 27,290 captives of Israel with him. They were the cream of Israel's citizens—her artisans, aristocrats, and learned men. As was his custom, Sargon scattered the captives throughout his empire. This scattering of Israel is often referred to as "the ten lost tribes." Sargon brought colonists from other parts of the Assyrian empire to Israel and settled them in Samaria (II Kings 17:24). Their languages, religions, and different races made them "outsiders" for awhile; but as the years passed, intermarriage made them one people. They were not "one," however, to the elite of Judah. They were a hybrid race, had a hybrid language and hybrid religion—and therefore were unworthy to worship in the Temple in Jerusalem. These people became the hated "Samaritans" of the New Testament era. When Jesus referred to a "good Samaritan" the two words clashed with each other—how could a *Samaritan* be *good?* So thought the "blue bloods" of Judah!

The life of Israel, the northern kingdom, thus came to an abrupt end only two centuries after the great monarchy had been established by David and Solomon. However, the life of Judah continued for another century and a quarter.

The Kingdom of Judah

With the division of the kingdom, Judah became a very small country. However, she was a stable country—the Davidic dynasty ruling continuously for over three hundred years, except for the short period when Jezebel's daughter, Athaliah, ruled. Judah was more isolated than Israel, being in the hill country, a fact which helps to account for its provincialism as compared with the more cosmopolitan Israel. The continuity of the Davidic dynasty assured the country that political anarchy would not engulf the land as was the case in Israel. In Israel there were nine different dynasties with nineteen rulers!

With the division of the kingdom, civil war ravaged

Palestine, to the great hurt of both states. Rehoboam feared to engage in war because of prophetic counsel against it. But when his grandson, Asa, became king, he went so far as to bribe Ben-hadad, king of Syria, to break his treaty with Israel and attack Israel, which Ben-hadad did!

Finally, Israel and Judah found peace together during the prosperous years when Jeroboam II ruled Israel and Uzziah ruled Judah—a reign that lasted for approximately forty years. Under the leadership of Uzziah (Azariah), Judah extended her borders in the west, south, and east. Uzziah forced the Philistines into an even narrower strip along the coast, forced the Ammonites to pay tribute, and opened a trade route to Elath on the Gulf of Aqabah, where he developed a commercial port. King Uzziah strengthened the fortifications of Jerusalem, improved his country's military defenses, and helped create a fresh interest among his people in agriculture and animal husbandry.

In the year that King Uzziah died (742 B.C.), Isaiah began to denounce the sins of luxury and soft living (Is. 2:6-9; 3:1-23; 5:7). He also denounced injustice; the tyranny of vice; the demoralizing effect of foreigners at court, of corrupt national leaders, and of immoral and ungodly religion. During his long ministry, Isaiah had witnessed the anarchy of Israel and the lack of faith in Judah. In 734 B.C. he had an appointment with King Ahaz to reassure him about the war which Pekah of Israel and Rezin of Syria were preparing to wage against him because of his refusal to enter their coalition against Assyria. Isaiah urged him to an act of faith:

> If you will not believe,
> surely you shall not be established (Isa. 7:9).

But Ahaz had already sent a gift to the Assyrian monarch, Tiglath-pileser, asking him to wage war against Israel and Damascus. Tiglath-pileser attacked and ravaged the land, capturing Galilee, the plain of Esdraelon, Gilead, Philistia, and sections of Arabia.

Ahaz was summoned to Damascus to report to "Pul" [2] as his vassal, and pay fealty to him. Ahaz, observing the altar set up at Damascus, assumed that the Assyrian's religion and god was mightier than that of Yahweh. So he ordered that the worship of Assyria's deities be substituted for worship at Solomon's Temple, and he implemented his ideas by setting up an Assyrian altar in Solomon's Temple in Jerusalem (II Kings 16:10-18). Little wonder that King Ahaz did not respond well to Isaiah's suggestion that he have faith in God! Nor would the king have been interested in the "sign" which Isaiah said would be proof that Yahweh would save him and his nation (Isa. 7:14).

We look in vain for some word from Isaiah about the fall of Israel in 721 B.C. He had seen its destruction, but not a word of gloating over its fall escaped his lips! Not once did he say, "I told you so." Undoubtedly he wept, as Amos had done before him!

Ten years later Isaiah, though an aristocrat, went about Jerusalem dressed as a slave (which means he went practically naked) for three years. He was saying in dramatic form, more eloquent than speech, that if Judah put her faith in Egypt and Philistia in a proposed rebellion against Assyria, all her people would be captured and taken as slaves to Assyria (Isa. 20:1-6). He was correct, too! Sargon of Assyria sent his cavalry on Ashdod, delivering a smashing defeat to the Philistine forces, and Egypt proved to be but a reed in the wind!

The severest trial for Judah and Isaiah came in 701 B.C. when Sennacherib sent his forces against Hezekiah. Sennacherib's cylinder tells how he captured forty-six strongholds and fortresses of Judah and then shut Hezekiah up "like a bird in a cage" in Jerusalem. Isaiah had called for freedom from entangling alliances, fidelity to the nation's

---

[2] The Old Testament writers refer to Tiglath-pileser as "Pul," apparently a nickname, or at least an abbreviation of his name.

pledged word to Assyria, and fidelity to Yahweh. He argued that trust in the forces of Egypt was ill-placed, for this meant finding security in men rather than God and in horses (which were flesh) rather than spirit (Isa. 30:1-17; 31:1-9). Isaiah argued that Jerusalem, with Solomon's Temple within, was inviolable; it would not be taken; indeed, the Assyrians would stop their siege and return home. And this came to pass, too. Some consider that the bubonic plague, brought by hordes of mice from Egypt (as reported by Herodotus), saved Judah. The Judeans interpreted the lifting of the siege as another example of the redeeming grace of God.

The prophecies of Micah were heard at this time, too, about 701 B.C. The sufferings of the poor people in the lowlands is seen in his messages (Mic. 3:1-4) and his condemnation of the rapacious rich in Jerusalem who seemed to make money during times of warfare (Mic. 3:9-12).

Seventy-five years later, about 628 B.C., Jeremiah was called to his ministry. During his lifetime he witnessed the invasions of the Scythians, who helped create the conditions that led to the fall of the hated capital, Ninevah, of Assyria, 612 B.C., and the complete downfall of Assyria in 605 B.C. Jeremiah also witnessed and partook of the Deuteronomic reform of 621 B.C. under the leadership of Josiah, though he soon learned that goodness and godliness cannot be legislated! So he dreamed of a time when the covenant of God would be written, not on tablets of stone, but in the hearts of men (Jer. 31:31-33).

Jeremiah also witnessed and prophesied against the pro-Egyptian alliances of Jehoiakim, predicting ruin for Jerusalem and exile for her inhabitants. Jeremiah was branded a traitor and would have been killed had it not been for the leaders' memories of Micah (Mic. 3:12), who had said the same thing a hundred years earlier. But with a sad heart Jeremiah witnessed the invading forces of Nebuchadnezzar in 597 B.C. and the removal of ten thousand of Judah's citizens as slaves for Babylonia!

CHAPTER 5

The Postexilic Period

NEBUCHADNEZZAR CAPTURED Jerusalem twice, first in 597 B.C., and then in 587 B.C. The second time he completely destroyed the City of David (Jerusalem) with all its government buildings, palaces, and Solomon's Temple. On both occasions Nebuchadnezzar took exiles to Babylonia. The centuries following the destruction of Jerusalem in 587 B.C. are known as the postexilic period in the history of Judah.

The Babylonian Period

The bitterness of the exiles captured by Nebuchadnezzar is vividly expressed in Ps. 137:

> By the waters of Babylon,
>> there we sat down and wept,
>> when we remembered Zion.
> On the willows there
>> we hung up our lyres.
> For there our captors
>> required of us songs,
> and our tormentors, mirth, saying,
>> "Sing us one of the songs of Zion!"
>> (Ps. 137:1-3)

In this psalm the Judean exiles en route to Babylonia are portrayed as weeping over their plight, taunted by their Babylonian captors, refusing to sing their "songs of Zion" to their tormentors, their hearts filled with hatred for their southern neighbors the Edomites. We do not know exactly

where these exiles were taken in Babylonia, though Ezra
2:59 mentions a few places from whence some exiles left
in later decades when they returned to Jerusalem with him
in 397 B.C. We do know that some Jews were taken to
Nippur, because Jewish names appear on tablets found in
the archives of the Babylonian bank and brokerage firm
of Murashu and Sons in the fifth century.

From some tablets found at Babylon, we know that
Jehoiachin, the former king of Judah who had been captured and exiled to Babylonia in 597 B.C. by Nebuchadnezzar, was receiving good treatment in that capital city.
As a matter of fact, he seems to have been considered king
of Judah even though in exile. Archaeologists have found
evidence that indicates that Eliakim was his "steward," that
is, he was in charge of Jehoiachin's property in Judah
while the king was in exile. If so, then Zedekiah was
more or less regent for Jehoiachin during this period.
Ernst Weidner of Berlin translated some of the three
hundred tablets found in the basement of the Hanging
Gardens of Babylon. Among them were lists of payments
of rations in oil and grain from the Babylonian government to captives (among whom Jehoiachin's name
appears, names of skilled workmen from many nations (undoubtedly some were Judeans), and names of five royal
princes of Jehoiachin (among other Judeans). In addition
to those who received royal rations are listed mariners, musicians, shipbuilders, craftsmen, horse-trainers, and others.

The conditions of the Jews in exile must have been very
distasteful to them, yet evidence is not lacking to support
the idea that they had a considerable amount of freedom,
though exiled. Jeremiah wrote to the exiles suggesting that
they settle down, marry and beget children, and "seek the
welfare of the city where I [God] have sent you into
exile, and pray to the Lord on its behalf, for in its welfare
you will find your welfare" (Jer. 29:7). There can be little
doubt but that the exiles took him very seriously—in fact
so seriously that most of them refused to return to Judah

decades later when Cyrus' decree gave them that privilege! Most of them had established themselves financially, agriculturally, socially, and religiously. They were content. Nonetheless, Jeremiah fully expected the exiles to return after "seventy years" (that is a period of time); he assumed that King Jehoiachin was the real king, and that his descendants would return, too (Jer. 28–29).

Nebuchadnezzar, a very wise and enlightened ruler, was succeeded by three unworthy men, whose brief reigns were known for their disorder. Finally, the noteworthy Nabonidus came to the throne. It is very interesting to recall that his mother had been captured by Nebuchadnezzar at Haran (home of Abraham), where she was high priestess of the moon god, Sin. Little wonder that Nabonidus spent much of his time rebuilding the temple at Haran. But he also rebuilt many other temples, following in the footsteps of Nebuchadnezzar in this regard. However, Nabonidus antagonized the priests of his capital city, Babylon. They believed he was trying to replace their state god, Marduk, with the moon god, Sin. So rebellion seethed deeply in their hearts.

Nabonidus finally placed his son, Belshazzar, in charge of matters of state while he campaigned, rebuilt various temples, and ruled the empire in the west. It is this same Belshazzar whom we meet in the book of Daniel, with the reference to the handwriting on the walls of the banquet hall in Babylon (Dan. 5).

With the rise of the Elamite (later called Persian) rule under Cyrus, the days of Babylonia were obviously limited. Two great prophets of the exile spoke out clearly at this time, calling for mental and physical preparation for a return to Judah. These men were Ezekiel and the unknown author of Isa. 40–55. (Since the writer of Isa. 40–55 is unknown, scholars simply refer to him as Second Isaiah, or II Isaiah). Ezekiel called for personal responsibility in both repentance and in action. He declared that God, whose "glory" had left Jerusalem at the time of the captivity in

587 B.C., was ready to return with the exiles to Mt. Zion, the City of David. The last eight chapters of Ezekiel call for the centralization of the Temple in the life of the community. If this were done, this priestly prophet declared, both national and personal security would be assured, morality would abound, and faith in God would be conducive to national peace.

Second Isaiah also dreamed of a return to Jerusalem. He was a prophet of hope. At no time did he condemn the exiles for their past actions or infidelity. He simply lifted up a vision of a great return for Israel under the providential care of Yahweh. It would be a kind of second Exodus! As the waters of the *Yam Suph* had been cleared for a highway for the Hebrews, so a highway would be constructed across the northern part of the Arabian desert for their return. His faith in the creative and redemptive purposes of God has never been excelled by any prophet. He knew the historical events of his day—a time in which nations were falling and crumbling, new powers were arising, new demands were being made by enslaved people who were calling for their rights as persons, new questions concerning the validity of the exiles' faith in God were being raised. Yet Second Isaiah interpreted these historical events against the background of the activity of the concerned and redeeming God. God was active in human affairs. Second Isaiah even considered Cyrus the Great as a servant or anointed one ("Messiah" in Hebrew) of the Lord. It is most interesting to realize that Second Isaiah could see God's activity as being realized through the very people who were the overlords of the exiles.

An institution of great historical significance was developing during the early years of the postexilic period, namely, the rise of the synagogue. The exiles could not offer sacrifices in Jerusalem, nor could they offer sacrifices to Yahweh while exiled in Babylonia. The Deuteronomic Reform of 621 B.C. had forbidden offering sacrifices at any shrine other than at Solomon's Temple. As a substitute for sacrifices, the priests developed the customs and rituals of memorials. The exiles gathered together at festival times and related the "mighty acts of God" in their behalf in former times. This "meeting together" is the basic meaning of the word "synagogue." In time, the Jewish people built synagogues in every part of the world where there were enough Jewish men to warrant such a house. There were many synagogues in Jerusalem in Jesus' day, but there was only one Temple. The only other Jewish temple we know about was built in Egypt, on the island of Elephantine, near Aswan, Egypt, in the fifth century B.C.

Eventually, through the labors of both Ezekiel and Ezra, a century later than Ezekiel, the foundations were laid for the great emphasis on *obedience* to the Law. Thus was formed Judaism. We should remember that the basic ideas for Judaism arose in the hearts of exiles living in Babylonia. So this period is exceedingly important in the development of both Judaism and Christianity.

The Persian Period

Nabonidus' great interest in the moon god, Sin, developed not only animosity but also treason among the priests of Marduk, the state god of Babylonia. Cyrus, who had already taken over the kingdom of Media (550 B.C.), and conquered the fabulously rich Croesus, king of Lydia (546 B.C.), was practically handed the key to Babylon by its priesthood (539 B.C.)

It was in this period (540-538 B.C.) that Second Isaiah prophesied and even referred to Cyrus as God's servant, his chosen, his anointed (Isa. 42:1; 45:1). Cyrus was not only a great military man but also a great statesman. He reversed the Assyrian and Babylonian policies toward conquered people by issuing a decree that permitted all exiles, of all nations, to return to their native lands and to reestablish the religions of their homelands. Under this decree the exiles of Judah were also permitted to return to their native land of Judah and to reestablish worship at Jerusalem. This decree is described on the cylinder of Cyrus and in the book of Ezra (1:2-4; 6:3-5).

A comparatively small group did return to Judah under the leadership of a man of Davidic descent, named Sheshbazzar. He was replaced by his nephew, Zerubbabel, about 522 B.C. Under the prophetic activity of Haggai and Zechariah, the Temple was rebuilt in Jerusalem about 520-516 B.C. Many thought that Zerubbabel would be the long awaited "anointed one" (Messiah) who would restore the monarchy. But he was removed from office on order of the Persian ruler, Darius I, who appointed a governor to govern Judah. Judah became a part of the fifth *satrapy* (division) of the Persian Empire.

Of no small historical interest is the fact that Cyrus the Great and his successors, such as Darius and Xerxes, were all followers of Zoroaster. They worshiped Ahura-mazda, the god of light. Though they could think of God as the god of light, they seldom conceived of God as one of love. Their emphasis was on justice and truth, rather than mercy. Nonetheless we cannot help but wonder at the possible borrowing of metaphors when we read of the Jewish exiles returning to Palestine with the conviction that they are to be a *"light* for the Gentiles," and that their task is to help all mankind learn of the one true God.

It is also of interest to observe the fact that the Persians, following the new device created by the Greeks, began to mint coins. Previously, "money" was weighed out on scales, but now coins stamped with an image of the king began to appear.

Under Artaxerxes I (465-424 B.C.), Nehemiah returned to Jerusalem with royal permission to restore the waste places of Jerusalem. He achieved his goal, though faced with much opposition from Sanballat (governor of Samaria), Tobiah (of Ammon), and Geshem (of Edom and Arabia).

The governors, Sanballat and Tobiah, referred to in

Neh. 4:1-3, are also referred to in the Elephantine papyrus of this period. This document requests permission to re-build a Jewish temple on the island of Elephantine, near Aswan, Egypt. A reply to this letter has been found granting permission but with the stipulation that no animals be sacrificed, possibly because Deuteronomy states that animals are to be offered only in Jerusalem, or possibly because the Zoroastrians did not approve of violating fire, their sacred symbol, by the burning of animals. A "Passover Papyrus" dated a decade earlier grants permission to observe the Passover, but only according to precise regulations, which seem to be based on, or are at least in accord with, those of the Pentateuch.

These papyri are helpful to us because they reflect the concerns of Jews who lived in Egypt in the fifth century B.C. The Jewish inhabitants of Elephantine formed a military garrison on the island. Their interests were similar to those who lived in Palestine. Nehemiah's emphasis on racial and religious purity seems to have taken hold.

Ezra came to Palestine from Persia ("Babylonia," as it was called a century earlier) about 397 B.C. He came under the authority of the king, Artaxerxes II (405-359 B.C.), and established a political structure based on Jewish religious laws. The official language of the Persian Empire was Aramaic, which is the language Ezra used, judging by some of the passages in the book bearing his name (Ezra 4:8–6:18; 7:12-26). Ezra was appointed secretary for Jewish re-ligious affairs by Artaxerxes II with authority to establish civil obedience and demand religious reforms. Ezra called the Judeans (and apparently the Samaritans too) together and read to them the Law, possibly portions of the Penta-teuch or some exposition of the Mosaic law. The Jews ac-cepted these statutes and requirements. Stern measures were made concerning intermarriages also—with a consequent growing schism between Samaritans and Judah. When the schism did come, the Samaritans accepted the Torah—the Pentateuch, the first five books of the Old Testament—

but no more. By 400 B.C. the Judeans had also accepted the prophets as canonical scripture.

During the next few decades little is known about the political and religious activities of Judah. It is likely that parts of Joel, Zechariah, and possibly Isa. 19:1-15 were given by unknown prophets at this time and added to the prophetic scrolls.

The Greek Period

Alexander the Great (336-323 B.C.) attempted to conquer the world. His goal, perhaps on the advice of his learned teachers, among whom was Aristotle, was to unite the culture of Greece and those native to the lands he conquered. In a sense, his goal was a missionary one, for he wanted a united world under one language and under the dominant intellectual influence of Greek thought and knowledge. We readily admit that Aristotle had left a legacy of knowledge that the world needed. His interests were found in almost every discipline, such as geography, mathematics, medicine, metallurgy, biology, botany, logic, philosophy, and religion. Most plants and animals carry Greek names even today. The basic rules of logic, mathematics, drama, and art came from his creative mind.

Shortly after the capture of Issus in 333 B.C. the Persian Empire lost Palestine to the Greek armies led by Alexander. Alexander, however, died in Babylon in less than a decade, after failing to conquer India. His great empire was divided into three parts, two of which concern Old Testament studies: the Seleucid and Ptolemaic empires. The Seleucids controlled Asia Minor, Syria, and Babylon, and claimed Palestine; the Ptolemies claimed Egypt and Palestine. Palestine, therefore, became an uncertain boundary between these two Greek powers for a number of years—until 198 B.C. when the Seleucids seized the land and attempted to unite it with Syria under Hellenistic culture. During the next few decades, and especially under the reign of the

Seleucid king, Antiochus IV (175-164 B.C.), Judah faced great divergencies of opinion concerning her Greek overlords. Many saw no difficulty in mixing their Hebrew religion, language, literature, sports, and dress with that of the Greeks. Great amphitheaters, coliseums, theaters, colonnaded public buildings, and cultural activities found their way into the social life of Palestine. There was also staunch resistance, however, especially when Antiochus IV outlawed Judaism, denying Jews the right to read the scriptures on pain of death, refusing Jews the right to circumcise their infant sons on pain of having each baby killed and hung round his mother's neck for several days, outlawing the observance of the Sabbath and the dietary laws concerning clean and unclean foods. In 168 B.C. the Temple was desecrated by offering swine on the altar. Furthermore, the altar seems to have been dedicated to Zeus.

Pious Jews rose up in righteous wrath against such an abuse of religious rights. Their manner of rebellion differed with each person or group of persons. Some Jews preferred to die rather than to break the Torah and literally gave their lives for their faith (I Macc. 1, and II Macc. 6). Some wrote tracts to encourage others to be loyal even unto death—as was the case with the wonderful stories in the first few chapters of Daniel. Some simply prayed and hoped that God would act in their behalf. Still others decided that it was better to have faithful Jews alive who could worship God than to have a cemetery full of dead Jews who could no longer worship. So a group of pious Jews led what we know as the Maccabean revolt.

Some Jews collaborated with the Hellenists; others rebelled against them; while still others were loyal to their Hebrew faith, yet listened with open mind to Greek ideas. Such men wrote the remarkable synthesis of Greek ideas about creative logos in Prov. 8:22-31. Hebrew scholars translated the Hebrew Bible (composed of the Pentateuch— that is, Torah—and the prophets) into Greek, calling it the Septuagint (about 250 B.C.).

Jewish Independence

With the Maccabean revolt in 168 B.C. a war of independence was begun by the Jews, and they actually won their independence from Greek domination! Their new state maintained freedom for a little over a century, until the coming of the Roman, Pompey, in 63 B.C. With the capture of Jerusalem the Maccabeans rededicated the Temple in a ceremony of "lights." The light symbolized the Law. This festival is still observed by Jews and is called *Hanukkah* (feast of lights).

The Jewish state was considerably different from that of the Davidic monarchy. The Maccabeans, who led the revolt, were of a priestly family. The successors of the leader Judas Maccabeus assumed the title of king, and later that of high priest. Thus, both offices were combined in one person—even though the Maccabean family was not in the high-priestly line.

In this historic period two significant religious parties developed: the Pharisees and Sadducees. When the Maccabeans revolted against the Seleucid (Greek) Antiochus IV in 168 B.C., these Jewish religious revolutionaries were called Hasidim ("Pious Ones"). They were ready to die for their faith and for freedom to observe the rites and festivals of their faith. After the Maccabean revolution was over, however, the basic concerns of most were met, for they were basically interested in religion, not politics. Some of the *Hasidim,* on the other hand, did interest themselves in politics, even though they had "set themselves apart" (which is the translation of the word "Pharisee") from both the Greeks and Greek-loving Jews. Though greatly interested in obedience to their religious law, these Pharisees also were interested in evangelizing the heathen, in enlarging the canon of their Scripture, and in helping the masses to know God. These Pharisees were in large measure responsible for the enlargement of the canon to include the "Holy Writings" (such as Psalms, Proverbs, Jonah, Esther).

The Sadducees, obtaining their name from David's chief priest, Zadok, represented the priestly aristocracy. They were the ruling class during the Maccabean period. They are often referred to as the Hasmonaean dynasty. The Sadducees and the Samaritans accepted only the Pentateuch as Scripture. They were not really interested in the masses (much less the heathen Gentiles) and, unlike the Pharisees, they did not believe in a resurrection.

It was during the Pharisees' ascendancy to power under the reign of Alexandra, the first woman to rule the Jews [1] in all their history, that the system of required elementary schooling was established (about 75 B.C.). Education has been a basic requirement of Jews throughout all the centuries since that date.

Finally the strife between these two factions, the Sadducees and Pharisees, led to the annexation of Palestine by Rome under Pompey in 63 B.C. Soon Herod the Great, exploiting the Hasmonaean dissension, received from Rome the title of king. This Idumean (that is, Edomite) was ruthlessly cruel, even though he gave an outer splendor to Palestine never before known to that country. He died in 4 B.C., shortly after the birth of Jesus, a son born to Mary of Nazareth, of Galilee. [2]

With Herod's death his kingdom was divided into three parts and was governed for a time by each of his three sons —Archelaus, Antipas, and Philip.) Deep divisions grew ever wider, however, until a revolt by the Jews broke out in A.D. 66. Its fanaticism was so bitter and the Jews were so passionately loyal to the Temple ritual that Titus was forced to attack and sack the city of Jerusalem, destroying it completely. Of course, the new Temple was destroyed too. The table of shewbread was taken from the Temple, as were

[1] Athaliah, daughter of Ahab and Jezebel, was the first woman to rule over Judah. Strictly speaking, Athaliah did not rule over "the Jews" because this title was not given the Judeans until their exile in Babylon, about 587 B.C. Hence, Alexandra was the first woman to rule over the "Jews."

[2] Due to an error of an early calendar-maker our calendar is off by five years. When this book was published (1965), we were really living approximately in the year 1970 (1965 plus 5 years for needed correction).

the golden candlesticks and a roll of the Torah—all taken to Rome by Titus as trophies of war. Eventually the Apostle Paul undertook to explain how this very Torah (the Law of the first five books of the Old Testament) was fulfilled in Jesus of Nazareth, whom God had made the Christ by his resurrection from the dead.

Part II

THE LITERATURE
OF THE OLD TESTAMENT

WE HAVE NOTED the great achievements of the Near East—
the fabulous temples and palaces of Mesopotamia and
Egypt, the metal work of Sumer and Akkad, the customs
of Amorites, Hurrians, and Canaanites. Added to these
achievements of the people of the "Bible lands" were the
literary developments—the rituals, hymns, and liturgy of
these lands.

When Joshua led the children of Israel into Canaan,
they were faced with a very old and highly developed culture. Canaan had developed three systems of writing, one
of which was adopted by the Hebrews and eventually by
the Greeks, Romans, and our own civilization. The invading Hebrews came into contact with a culture which had
developed and codified its laws—in fact, Israel borrowed
from the Canaanites the social legislation of Exod. 21–23.
Israel also borrowed much of her wisdom literature from
Canaan, though some had its roots in Egypt. There can be
no question but that the Hebrews learned from the
Canaanites how to write psalms (hymns), in addition to ac-
quiring the very names and usages of many of their festivals.
The long-lost Canaanite library at Ras Shamra has been
found and translated, greatly enriching our knowledge as

to the intellectual and cultural climate of the period when the Israelites came into Canaan from Egypt in search of a homeland. It is more than interesting to learn that the Canaanites called God "El," as did the Hebrew patriarchs. She gave Israel its alphabet, and much of its religious symbolism.

Besides the cultural climate mentioned above, the Hebrews also brought with them many stories which their ancestors probably brought from ancient Ur and/or Haran: stories of the flood, of the creation of the world and of man, of the towers of Babel, and of the beginning of sin.

As a nomadic people, the Hebrews listened to story-tellers when the elders of the clans gathered around the evening campfires. The storytellers, or minstrels, told of the experiences of the patriarchs Abraham, Isaac, and Jacob. After the former slaves left Kadesh-barnea, these storytellers added to their repertory such stories as the mighty acts of Yahweh who had appeared to Moses on Mt. Sinai (or Horeb, Exod. 3:1-6) and ordered the release of his chosen people from bondage in Egypt. They told of their deliverance by the hand of Yahweh from the Sea of Reeds, of God's providential care on their trek to Kadesh-barnea—the provision of quail, water from the rock, and manna on the tamarisk trees. They told of Moses receiving the "ten words" on Mt. Sinai, of building the Tabernacle, of Moses' meeting Yahweh at the tent of meeting, of the wilderness experiences at Kadesh-barnea, and of their trek from this oasis to the hills of Moab, where Moses died and Joshua took command.

Israel had a great literary heritage of her own when she arrived in the land of Canaan, a land of great literature and religious hymnody and ritual. The writers of Israel's literature depended on both the traditions which they themselves knew by heart and the knowledge of literature which they borrowed from peoples of other nations.

Our Scriptures therefore have an international flavor.

The basic sources of Gen. 2–11 come from Sumer and Akkad via the Amorites and Hurrians. Isa. 16–17 comes from an ancient Moabite. Part of Ps. 104 is a firm echo of the beautiful Hymn of Aton from the lips of the Egyptian monotheist, Akh-en-Aton. Prov. 22:17–23:14 is a revision of the Egyptian maxims of Amen-em-ope. The social legislation of Exod. 22–23, 34 was borrowed from the Canaanites, as also some of the civil legislation of Exod. 21–22. Much of the wisdom literature (possibly Job, Prov. 30:1–31:19, and so forth) apparently came to Israel from Edom. Needless to say, these non-Israelite literary documents were re-edited by the Hebrews when they wrote their own literature so that they reflected their own theological insights into the nature of God.

The Uniqueness of Israel

The uniqueness which Israel brought to the literary world was her insight into the meaning of history. As Israel reflected on her past, she was convinced that God had been acting in history in her behalf. The literature which she wrote (much of which we have in our Old Testament) was a varied attempt to show that God acted redemptively out of love for his chosen people. So her hymnody (though constructed from a Canaanite style of poetry) was concerned with her praise to Yahweh, her redeeming God. Her wisdom literature, though much borrowed from Canaan and Egypt, was centered on the "fear of the Lord" as the basis for true wisdom. Her historical records were more than history; they were narratives that illustrated the providence of God in behalf of his people. Even her songs (whether love, taunt, funeral, or dirge) were couched in her faith. Likewise Israel's social and civil legislation, though borrowed to some extent from Canaan and Mesopotamia, was re-edited by an astute and pious writer who put the laws in the context of his faith in the Lord of history.

Possible Methods for Study of Literature of the Old Testament

There are several approaches that can be used in the study of the literature of Israel. One approach is to analyze the various types of literature that compose the Old Testament. This approach recognizes the fact that the Old Testament is a library in the real sense of that word. This library contains thirty-nine books. These books were written by persons over a span of eight hundred years—from about 930 to 100 B.C. They were written for the most part in Hebrew, though portions of some (as in Ezra and Daniel) were written in Aramaic. (The New Testament was written in Greek.) The types of literature which are found in this library include history, law, short stories, genealogies, poetry, hymns, secular and religious songs, prophetic oracles, riddles, fables, devotional materials, wisdom literature, and apocalypse.

Though recognizing the value of the above types, the approach in this book is chronological. This is done so that the reader can think of the various writings against the historical background out of which they came. For example, when we study prophetic oracles, we will state the date of the prophet being studied so that the reader can refer back to Part I for the historical setting of that period. We will use this same chronological approach for Part III, the theological study of the Old Testament.

The Earliest Writings of the Old Testament

Before starting our study, it might be well to say a word about the canonization of the Bible. Though the first document to be written was very likely the historical writings about King David found in II Sam. 9–16 and dated about 930 B.C., and though Amos was the first book to be completed in the form in which it now appears (about 760 B.C.), it is commonly recognized that the book of Deuteronomy, written sometime prior to 621 B.C., was the first book that was considered the Word of God.

Though Deuteronomy was the first to be recognized as the Word of God, there were other scrolls which described the faith of Israel. Among these very early documents are two basic ones which we know as the northern account of the history of Israel and the southern account of the history of Judah. Each of these histories was concerned with the same theme: God's election of Israel and his providential care over his people from the days of Abraham, through the experiences of bondage and release from Egypt, to the final conquest of Canaan. Though the two accounts deal with the same events, their telling of the story often varies considerably. The accounts differ according to the perspective of the writer. This may be illustrated in this way: Suppose a very conservative Northerner and a conservative Southerner were each writing an account of the American Civil War. The details of many battles would vary according to the perspectives of the writers. So it was with the accounts which told of God's activity in behalf of Israel.

The southern account has come to be known as the "J tradition," partly because the major use of the divine name is "Yahweh," [1] and also because "J" represents Judah, the southern kingdom. The northern account is referred to as the "E-tradition," partly because the word for God is "Elohim," and also because "E" represents Ephraim, the northern kingdom.

Many scholars are convinced that eventually these two historical traditions were combined into one tradition (or document), which we may call JE. After Deuteronomy (D) had been written and later discovered and accepted as scripture (621 B.C.), another historical tradition came into being in the late fifth century B.C. It was centered in the priestly point of view rather than a specifically northern

---

[1] The divine name is so written in Hebrew that it cannot be pronounced. The KJV translated it in some places as "Jehovah," though it should be pronounced "Yahweh."

or southern point of view. This priestly tradition has sometimes been given the name "Priestly Code" and is often
referred to as the "P-document." Apparently the priestly
circle (or individual) used their own tradition as the basic
outline for the history of Israel. Into this outline were
drawn the materials of the other traditions—J, E, and D.
The result was a composite tradition (symbolized as JEDP
by scholars) which we know as the Pentateuch—that is,
the first five books of the Old Testament. The Jews refer
to it as the Torah (the Law).

The writers of our Old Testament refer to twenty-four
different books (none of which exist today) which were
used as source materials for the writing of the books of
the Bible as we have them today. For example, the writers
used the book of Jashar, the chronicles of the Kings of
Judah, the chronicles of the Kings of Israel, the chronicles
of various temples, and so forth. In short, some of the
writers of the Old Testament wrote their books in the
same manner described in Luke 1:1-4. The writers got all
the information available first, then took reed in hand and
recorded on papyrus their findings, still interpreting and
perhaps even modifying in accord with their particular
points of view.

The Canonization of Books
of the Old Testament

Within a decade or two after the Pentateuch received its
present form it was accepted as authoritative for faith. This
means that the Pentateuch was canonized—accepted by
the community and religious leaders as the standard expression of the will of God for man and permissible for
use in services of worship. This great event took place
about 400 B.C.

Two centuries later, about 200 B.C., a second group of
scrolls was accepted as authoritative—the Prophets. This
group included the former prophets (the historical writ-

ings, found in Joshua, Judges, I and II Samuel, and I and II Kings), and the latter prophets (Isaiah, Jeremiah, Ezekiel, and the twelve minor prophets).

The four historical scrolls—Joshua, Judges, Samuel and Kings—had been in circulation since 550 B.C. The four scrolls of the latter prophets (Isaiah, Jeremiah, Ezekiel, and the Twelve) were accepted as canonical scripture about 200 B.C. In this connection it is interesting to read the book of Chronicles and recall the fact that the writer lived at a time (possibly about 250 B.C.) when the four historical books were not considered to be scripture, hence, he could take great liberties with the content of the scrolls. A casual reading will quickly indicate this fact. By 180 B.C. Ben Sira referred to his Bible as "The Law and the Prophets." [2] This is also the Bible which Jesus would have known.[3] The Holy Writings (which included such books as the Proverbs, Psalms, Jonah, Ruth, and so forth) although they enjoyed varying degrees of authority and influence, were not canonized until the Council of Jamnia (A.D. 90). Therefore, they were not accepted as scripture by Jesus, but since the Christians adopted the Jewish Bible as formulated at the Council of Jamnia, we include the Holy Writings in our Christian Scriptures too.

Let us now study in chronological order, the literature of Israel, our Old Testament.

---

[2] See the Prologue to the apocryphal book The Wisdom of Sirach (Ecclesiasticus).
[3] Compare with Luke 16:29.

CHAPTER 1

Pre-Monarchic Literature

THE WRITTEN LITERATURE of Israel began to come into existence after 1000 B.C. with the rise of the monarchy. Prior to that time traditions were transmitted orally. Of course, there were a few exceptions, as we shall realize.

But, first, let us note some of the literature that was transmitted orally in the days prior to the monarchy. Some of the literature was in the form of songs. These were sometimes communal in nature, sometimes private.

Many of the communal songs, which were written down scores of years after being handed down orally, were songs of joy. Among these are such songs as the Song of Miriam (Exod. 15:21), and the triumphal ode of Deborah (Judg. 5). Both of these songs praise Yahweh for his redemptive activity in Israel's behalf against her enemies. A song used in the digging of a well is found in Num. 21:17-18:

> Spring up, O well!—Sing to it!—
> the well which the princes dug,
> which the nobles of the people delved,
> with the scepter and with their staves.

The proud and arrogant song of the bloodthirsty Lamech, who would avenge seventy times seven (Gen. 4: 23-24), is perhaps what Jesus had in mind when he said that we are to forgive seventy times seven. Lamech's song is certainly an ancient poem. Lamech represents the first delinquent produced by a progressive, but religionless culture.

Note also the battle song of Joshua in Josh. 10:12b-13a, which is not to be read as prose, but as poetry:

76

> Sun, stand thou still at Gibeon,
> and thou Moon in the valley of Aijalon.
> And the sun stood still, and the moon stayed,
> until the nation took vengeance on their enemies.

Besides the communal songs there were also private songs to be sung by individuals. The Song of Songs was originally sung by an individual as he sang about his loved one. Though of late origin, these songs reflect ancient folk songs sung during courtship or at wedding festivities. Riddles were sometimes put in verse form at weddings (compare with Judg. 14:14, 18). Ancient banquet songs in the spirit of

> "Let us eat and drink,
>   for tomorrow we die"

were sung by the revelers (Isa. 22:13; compare with Wisd. of Sol. 2:6-9).

There were also private songs of blessings or good wishes. Newlyweds received blessings from their friends (Ruth 4: 11-22); good wishes were given to a bride as she left her father's home (Gen. 24:60), and fathers bestowed blessings on their sons (Gen. 27:27-29, 39-40; 49).

The opposite of private songs of love or blessings were private taunts as seen in II Kings 2:23. From these personal taunts developed political taunt songs, such as used by Isaiah (23:16) and by Second Isaiah, who personified Babylon as a woman of ill repute (Isa. 47).

Prior to 1000 B.C., in the pre-monarchic period, there was some written as well as oral literature. The Canaanites had social and civil laws which had been written for many decades, some of which are reflected in Exod. 21–23. Some Canaanite hymns had been written by 1400 B.C. and were preserved by being buried in their library where they remained until archaeologists discovered them centuries later.

Most significant of all, however, were the "ten words" (as the Old Testament usually refers to the Ten Commandments) which Moses received on Mt. Sinai. We have indicated previously how wise Moses was in his use of current Hittite suzerainty treaties for the basic form of the Ten Commandments. Now we note that these were written down and thus become a part of the great literature of the age.

Some of the most significant literature of Israel was developed in creedal form at Shechem during these early days. The confessional creeds of Deut. 26:2-10 and Josh. 24 were formulated and memorized during the period of the judges. These creeds became the guidelines for most of the future writings of Israel, for they held high the faith that Yahweh was the Lord of history and that he had chosen them, redeemed them from slavery, and given them the land of Canaan for an inheritance. Though these two creeds were not written down for several centuries, they were nonetheless exceedingly important to the future life of the people of Israel.

CHAPTER 2

The Literary Renaissance of the Monarchy

DAVID AND SOLOMON were the only two kings to rule over all Israel. King Saul was more of a rustic tribal chieftain than a king, though he used that title. Saul ushered in the concept of a monarchy, which resulted in a national renaissance, but he never actually ruled the entire land of Palestine as David was to do, nor did he have a great palace, collect taxes, or rid the land of its enemies. With Solomon's death, the monarchy was split in twain, so Solomon's son, Rehoboam, ruled over only a portion of the original monarchy. Rehoboam ruled over the small country of Judah, while Jeroboam, the king of the northern kingdom, ruled over Israel.[1]

Under the leadership of King David and King Solomon Israel entered an entirely new era, an era of intellectual, spiritual, and political enlightenment.

The soil in which the seeds of this new enlightenment grew was the development of the monarchy. When David became the monarch of both Israel and Judah, he changed the religious basis of Israel's life. In the days of the judges and of Saul the Israelites were bound together by worship at the tribal shrines, such as those at Shechem, Shiloh, Gilgal, Beersheba, and Bethel. The shrine which housed the Ark of the Covenant was considered the most sacred shrine. To that shrine annual pilgrimages were made, and there the confessional creeds (such as Deut. 26:5-10) were

---

[1] The northern kingdom was often referred to as Israel, Ephraim, and, later, Samaria.

79

recited, offerings were given, and prayers were made in behalf of the clans and the tribal confederacy. David, however, changed all of this by bringing the ark to Jerusalem, where he housed it.

A major problem was that Jerusalem, a former Canaanite city, had no religious heritage which called for pilgrimages for annual festivals. Since the religious questions of that period centered on the relevance of the faith of the fathers for the new day, the question was posed: If Jerusalem is the new religious center, should annual pilgrimages be made to Gibeon, to Bethel, and Gilgal? Is there any essential relationship between the festivals of the sacred shrines and the new sanctuary in Jerusalem?

Furthermore, the original division of the land of Canaan into the territories held by the twelve tribes was no longer deemed adequate. Instead, the land was divided into twelve new administrative districts, with administrative cities and an administrative officer over each city.

The old cultic basis for worship and unity seemed to be nullified, for all practical purposes. Israel was now a nation with a centralized government, a royal sanctuary, with royal priests appointed by the throne. Moreover, the royal priests were now financially supported by the throne, not by the offerings made by the people.

Added to these cultic innovations were the new innovations in the court—new palaces, government buildings, scores of new offices for new officers (royal secretaries, recorders, a commandant of the army, tax collectors, and so forth), and concerns about the state and public relations between it and other states. David (and Solomon, in much greater numbers) had entered marriages of state—assuring his country peace by the fact that his father-in-law would not go to war against him. Thus, many foreign faces in the harem and the embassies began to mingle with the people of Israel. A new cosmopolitan outlook in politics, economics, and religion swept over the land.

David is the first man known to have built an empire on

the eastern border of the Mediterranean. Formerly the land of Canaan had been conquered and annexed for purposes of taxation now by Egyptians, now by peoples from the north or northeast (Mesopotamians). His capital city was beautiful, his government well-organized. His official staff, patterned after that of Egypt, was efficient and orderly. His removal of the ark from Kiriath-jearim to his capital was a master stroke to centralize religious loyalties to his city.

It was in this period that the first book of Israel appeared. We find this book in what is now known as II Sam. 9–20 and I Kings 1–2.

The Father of History

The writer of II Sam. 9–20 and I Kings 1–2 was not the first to produce a written account of his king. Writers had done this concerning the great Thut-moses III, Ramses II of Egypt, the great Hittite king, Hattushil, early Mesopotamian kings, and others. The author of II Sam. 9–20, however, treated his material differently from the method of the Egyptian and Mesopotamian writers, who exaggerated without any ideal of objectivity or precision. For example, the inscriptions at Abu Simbel of Ramses II's war at Kadesh are certainly an unhistorical and untrustworthy source for scholars wishing to recreate the history of that period. But not so this material in II Samuel. It is of the highest type of historical literature. It is considered by some scholars to be unsurpassed in historicity, psychological insight, literary style, and dramatic power.

Robert H. Pfeiffer has argued quite logically that the writer of this first history of Israel was Ahimaaz, an eyewitness to the events which are recorded concerning his beloved King David.

Inasmuch as the writer of this first book of history had no model from which to draw any guidelines for writing, he has been given the title "the father of history." Writing either during the close of David's life or during the early reign of King Solomon, the writer is quite objective, even showing impartiality toward his hero, David. David is portrayed in his moments of chivalry, kindness, and religious enthusiasm; he is also portrayed in his moments of sin (in his order of the death of Uriah in order to marry Bathsheba) and in his willingness to join the Philistine king, Achish of Gath, in fighting against Saul. The author regarded the monarchy as a divine gift—in sharp contrast to Deuteronomy, Hosea, and the E-tradition.

The Masterpiece of Israel's History

Though the first book of Israel's history, referred to above, is highly valued for its excellent literary values (classical Hebrew, expert use of syntax, appropriate idioms, lively dialogues, and vivid descriptions), it seems likely that a decade or so later saw an even greater writer than the writer of part of II Samuel and I Kings. This is the Yahwist, the writer of what we call the J-document. His writing is the theological masterpiece of the Old Testament, for through his writings he met the grave theological crisis of his day, which his predecessor failed to do.

The Yahwist lived during the latter days of Solomon. He witnessed the changes from the old confederacy of twelve tribes to the new state, with its palaces, government buildings and officers, and its Temple. He also witnessed the growth of new interests in matters of the mind.

Solomon was a kind of Aristotle in his day, for he had encyclopedic knowledge of things round about him. I Kings 4 speaks of his wisdom in the appointments of officials of his court (secretaries, recorder, and so forth), his interest in horses (forty thousand stalls!), and his "largeness of mind like the sand on the seashore"—wiser than the wise men of Egypt. He was noted for his "three thousand proverbs" and his knowledge of trees, beasts, birds, reptiles, and fish. The wisdom by which he adjudicated legal cases or constructed chariot cities or developed copper mines and a navy at Ezion-geber on the Gulf of Aqabah or built his lovely Temple—all point to an age which was interested in man and what man could achieve.

Many in Israel had now developed a strong sense of history. This was one of their unique abilities. Israel looked at her past not as a series of fragmentary episodes but as the arena in which God's gracious acts were acted out in her behalf. The old creeds (see Deut. 26:5-10; Josh. 24) emphasized how God had redeemed the Israelites from slavery in Egypt and had saved them at the crossing of the Reed Sea. God had given them a covenantal relationship with him at Sinai, had cared for them in the Wilderness of Kadesh-barnea, and had finally given them the land of Canaan.

In the new age of intellectual interests of David's and Solomon's time, new concepts arose. God acted in behalf of his people not only through the miraculous events as recited in their creeds but also through more hidden ways —through the hearts of men. The Yahwist began to reinterpret the ancient covenantal faith of Israel in terms of the newer understanding of man. God's loving and saving acts are recognized as working through the motives of persons. His divine guidance is seen in the stories of the wooing of Rebecca, in which the servant receives inner assurance that God's guidance is being made known. This indirect method of the divine activity on Israel's behalf is seen in the deep sleep which Yahweh caused to come over Saul and his men—an act which gave aid to David (I Sam. 26:12). Joseph is guided throughout his life by this indirect method of God (Gen. 45:5-8; 50:20).

With this fresh insight into the fact that God acts through the heart of man as well as in the events of history, a new interest in religious understanding came into being. The Yahwist wrote from this new perspective. God is now viewed as moving not only in the sacred area of life but secular areas of life as well. So a new interest in man him-

self developed. For this reason we see concern for understanding such difficult psychological processes as the love
and hate experiences of Saul toward David; and the chilling
effect which the news that Joseph ruled in Egypt made on
the mind of Jacob ("And his heart fainted, for he did not
believe them"—Gen. 45:26).

The Yahwist was noted also for his lively dialogues. A
good example of this interest in rhetoric is in the dialogues
between Saul and David, recorded in I Samuel 24 and 26,
in which the anointed king, Saul, is humiliated before the
younger man, who has also been anointed and is to succeed
him.

All these interests—in the psychological processes within
man, proper speech, scientific interests of nature (as recorded in I Kings 4)—suggest that the Yahwist was writing
his masterpiece in an attempt to make the faith of the
fathers relevant for the new age of enlightenment in which
he lived.

It is quite possible that the Yahwist, though appreciative
of the new age of enlightenment, was also its (and Solomon's) strongest critic. He appreciated the progress of his
day, but it was made at a high price. As he observed King
Solomon proudly building palaces, government buildings,
the Temple, chariot cities, copper smelters, and a navy, he
realized that pride of what Solomon had achieved was a
major motivation. Solomon's marriages to many women led
him down the path of apostasy, for he built many shrines
to foreign gods at his wives' request. Many of their gods
were fertility deities and required "worship" which was
sensual and immoral. The royal harem was a veritable
"babel of voices," for the wives of many lands and their
children often spoke in their native tongues. Solomon, in his
attempt to "make a name for himself," conscripted labor
battalions from his own people in order to build and maintain his enterprises.

The Yahwist decided to use the ancient stories which his
ancestors (possibly Abraham) had brought from Ur and

Haran to awaken his age to the need for faith. So he refashioned the old traditions and put them in the form of remarkable parables. Thus, he spoke to Solomon's apostasy and his refusal to abide by the absolute standards of God by telling the parable of Adam and Eve, and the substitution of *their* (Adam's and Eve's) standards for the absolutes of God (Gen. 3). The Yahwist dealt with the pride of the capital city, with its new palaces, government buildings, marble columns, and Temple, by telling the story of Cain and his founding of the new city of Enoch. This city was noted (as was Jerusalem, under Solomon) for its use of iron, copper, and bronze; for its singing and music; for its musical instruments such as the lyre; for its fine arts; for its development of husbandry and its agricultural interests. But Cain's city lacked two major disciplines: morality and religion. The fruit of this city of religionless culture was Lamech, whose boast of hate and brutality must have shocked even Cain (Gen. 4:17-24).

The Yahwist dealt with the sensuality of the social and religious life of his day by telling the parable of Noah's flood, a judgment on another religionless and immoral culture (Gen. 6–8). Finally the Yahwist denounced the arrogance and pride which drove the monarch to "make a name for himself" by beautifying his city with buildings, especially his Temple, of polished granite and cedar from Lebanon. The Yahwist told of another culture whose people built their shrine on the top of a three-hundred-foot-high ziggurat in Babylon in an attempt to "make a name for themselves" (Gen. 11:1-9). The story showed that pride, even in the houses of worship which men build to God, can be the downfall of a culture. (We wonder how Solomon reacted to these stories.)

But these parables, told in an attempt to make the faith of the fathers relevant for 930 B.C., have eternal value, for they portray the basic sins of all men—the sins which separate men from God. We in our day are separated from both God and our fellowmen, indeed from ourselves, by pride, rebellion against God's absolutes, sensuality, and an immoral and often religionless culture. Thus the Yahwist speaks to our need too.

Having related God's creation of the world (Gen. 2) and the sinfulness of mankind (Gen. 3–11), the writer of the J-document then wrote of how God chose Abraham and his seed to save mankind.

The Yahwist gathered together all the oral traditions he could obtain and wove them together into the remarkable narratives of the patriarchal period (Gen. 12–50). The key point was the threefold promise to Abraham: (1) "I will make of you a great nation"; (2) "by you all the families of the earth will bless themselves"; (3) "to your descendants I will give this land [Canaan]" (Gen. 12:2-3, 7b).

The Yahwist wove these three promises and the traditions he knew concerning them into the basic historical document (the J-document) of the Old Testament. His writing was primarily an unfolding of the providential plan for the fulfillment of these three promises. Suspense, near tragedy, love, fear, hate—all give way under divine intervention. Using the three promises as the basic divisions of his work, the Yahwist presented the unfolding drama of God's gracious acts to Israel and through Israel to mankind. Expanding the earlier confessional creeds of Shechem (Deut. 26:5-10 and Joshua 24), the writer added to the creedal skeleton so that the events became flesh and the legendary characters walked and prayed on the written page. God's first and second promises were fulfilled in Egypt—Israel became a mighty nation, and through Israel many peoples were blessed by being saved from famine through Joseph, who was guided by God's care. The third promise was fulfilled after the Exodus from Egypt, with the conquest of the land of Canaan.

The Yahwist's account begins with creation, describes the conquest of Canaan, and concludes with the establishment of the monarchy under David. His point was to help his contemporaries realize that God's election of and covenant with Israel was still relevant for Solomon's age. He wanted his contemporaries to know that the God who created the world and acted in the events of their fore-father's history was still active in their time too—though his activity was being channeled through the inner lives of men as well as through the historical events of the past. He wanted his contemporaries to see that the God of the fathers—Abraham, Isaac, Jacob, Joseph, Moses, and Joshua —was also the God of David. Through God's new covenant with David and his dynasty, God's purposes would continue to be fulfilled for Israel and for mankind.

The J-document is superb in its concept of Yahweh as the Lord of history whose purposes continue through the present age. The writer lifted up a picture of a glorious future for Israel and thus helped develop a strong national-ism never before known by the nation.

CHAPTER 3

The Literature of the Divided Kingdom

THE LITERATURE of the divided kingdom—that written between the time of Solomon's death about 922 B.C. and the fall of the northern kingdom (Israel) in 721 B.C.—contains four major literary works: (1) the third historical document (the E-traditions); (2) Amos; (3) Hosea; and (4) Isaiah. (Isaiah began to prophesy in this period, but his ministry continued past 721 B.C.)

The E–Traditions

By the middle of the eighth century, both the northern and southern kingdoms were enjoying their heyday. At the death of Solomon, Jeroboam I had established a kingdom in the north and had set his capital at Shechem, where the ancient shrine of Israel had been located. He built national shrines at Bethel and Dan. There can be little doubt but that he continued to encourage annual pilgrimages to his capital city at Shechem, where the creeds (see Josh. 24) were recited, the covenant was renewed, offerings were given, and prayers were offered to Yahweh in behalf of all Israel.

A century later, Jeroboam II enjoyed a long and prosperous reign. He followed in the footsteps of his namesake, Jeroboam I, by urging worship at his royal temples at Dan and Bethel. Politically he was able to extend the borders of his country into Transjordan and to the north. Economically, he established commercial relations with other nations and brought in an age of economic prosperity. Religion "prospered" too, though in ways denounced by the austere herdsman from Tekoa, Amos. The royal sanctuaries were crowded on festival days, the priests were prospering financially, and most people seemed to be content. Religion and nationalism were too often bound together. To be religious was to be nationalistic, and vice versa. Many assumed that the luxury of the day was due to God's great love for Israel, even though apostasy was rampant.

Apparently, there were some northern priests who were discontented with the sacred records of the south, those formulated by the Yahwist (the J-document). There were points of view which needed to be corrected from a northern perspective; and there was not enough attention given to the northern shrines of Shechem, Bethel, and Penuel—all shrines of significance to Jacob, and hence to northerners. So, apparently, some concerned priests, seeing the inadequacies of their records, and also concerned with showing how the old faith of Israel was relevant for their day, decided to write their own history.

Since the word used for God in the E-tradition was for the most part "Elohim," [1] and since the northern country was often designated Ephraim, we find a good reason for using the symbol "E" for the history of the faith of northern Israel. The E-tradition was very similar to the J-tradition in many respects. When the J and E traditions were combined about 660 B.C., much of E was omitted, so that we do not have a continuous account of E in our present biblical material. There are often only fragments left, but there is enough that scholars have been able to analyze the E-tradition carefully.

They find that the author began with the threefold promises to Abraham (Gen. 15) and continued through Joshua. The account lacks the universal scope of J. It corrects the anthropomorphisms of J (having God speak not

---

[1] Elohim is pronounced: *El* (as in *el*evator)-*o-heem*. Recall that Yahweh was the name used for God in the J-document.

directly to man—as to Adam—but through visions or angels) and emphasizes the miraculous more than J. Ritual, sacrifice, and festivals at the northern shrines are emphasized. Writing classical Hebrew at its best, the author (or authors) lifted up a vision of a glorious future for the nation under the protection of God—even though this vision was refuted by history only thirty years later when Ephraim (Israel) was taken into captivity by Sargon II.

Nonetheless, the writer's deep intent was to reinterpret the faith in written form so that his contemporaries could be inspired to greater loyalty to Yahweh and to greater understanding of the faith for their new day of prosperity. His hope was based on God's steadfast love as expressed in his saving acts of mercy to the patriarchs, Moses, Joshua, and his chosen people. The priestly author of the E-tradition was convinced that God's actions in behalf of the Hebrews had not ceased; God would lead them to an even greater future.

The Book of Amos

The book of Amos contains the messages of a shepherd from Tekoa about 760 B.C. With the exception of the book of Isaiah, this book is unequaled in its purity of language and classical simplicity of style. Moreover, this literary ability is matched by the writer's theological ability. Amos was one of the truly great religious thinkers not only of his own day but of all time.

The reign of Jeroboam II brought an age of military security and economic affluence to Israel, the northern kingdom. Those merchants and speculators who profited from the victorious wars multiplied their offerings and sacrifices at the sanctuaries of Bethel and Gilgal (Amos 4:4-5; 5:5, 21-23). They interpreted these economic and military blessings as signs of God's special favor on them, concluding that they deserved these things because of their great offerings at the shrines.

Amos, called of God to preach, left his flocks at Tekoa (in Judah) and went to Bethel (in Israel, the northern kingdom) to voice his concern over the misunderstanding of God's will. He denied the assumption that God desired gifts, even though costly and numerous. Amos pointed out that God was interested, not primarily in the *act* of worship, but rather in the *life* of the worshiper. God wanted justice to be disbursed in the courts where now bribery of the judge was practiced. God wanted honesty in the market where false weights and false bottoms were being used. God wanted employers to face their responsibilities for the laborer who, being woefully underpaid, could not live on his wages.

Amos declared that God's primary concern was not in sacral acts, such as the giving of fine offerings, or reciting of creeds at annual pilgrimages to Shechem or Bethel; rather, God demanded that

"justice [should] roll down like waters,
and righteousness like an ever-flowing stream" (Amos 5:24).

Amos, expanding the concept of the Yahwist who wrote two centuries earlier, declared that Yahweh was the Lord of history—of all history, not only that of Israel. He declared that God was interested in all nations, loving the Negroes of Africa and the Philistines (Israel's national enemy) of Crete as much as he did the Israelites of Samaria (Amos 9:7). Needless to say, most of Amos' northern listeners were not ready to accept such a doctrine of God's universal concern.

Amos developed a theology of history which has been unsurpassed in our own times—a view which determined the framework to be used by the Deuteronomic writers when they wrote their histories, found in the books of Samuel, Judges, and Kings. Basically, Amos argued that God was active in history in his day, as surely as he had been active in the days of Abraham and Moses. God was working out his

purposes, but his purposes were greater than those of helping his chosen people obtain the land of Canaan. His
purposes were worldwide and were to be recognized by
peoples of all lands. By noting what Amos condemns in
chs. 1 and 2, we see that God's will was (and is) that all
peoples of all lands be just, compassionate, honorable,
trustworthy, moral, and faithful to the best they have
learned about God. Those nations who refused to live in
harmony with such moral demands would find that God's
moral order and their choices would bring them into conflict
with one another—that is, immoral nations inevitably war
with one another. Amos was saying: Peace is impossible between nations who refuse to live by the moral laws of God;
war is inevitable between those who refuse to live by justice,
compassion, honor, and obedience to God.

Amos was a religious revolutionary. He sought to enlarge
man's conception of God's own nature, God's interest in
all his peoples, God's ways of bringing peace or war (being
dependent on man's choices), and God's desires for a life
of right relationships (a life in which one's acts in worship
are consistent with a life of covenant obedience). Needless
to say, Amaziah, the high priest of this wealthy royal
sanctuary at Bethel, was not sympathetic to this herdsman's
sermons. He ordered Amos to leave the land of Israel (Amos
7:10-17). Back in Tekoa Amos or his disciples eventually
recorded his messages, and thus was formed the book of
Amos.

The Book of Hosea

Hosea may have come from a priestly family like that of
Jeremiah. He lived in Israel, in the tribe of Benjamin, just
north of the Judean border. Hosea probably heard the
herdsman from Tekoa preach at Bethel or somewhere else.
There are many verses in Hosea which show dependency on
the great insights of the Tekoan prophet.

Hosea's ministry was approximately from 747 to 735 B.C.

He lived during the time of Jeroboam II and witnessed the events in Israel against which Amos prophesied. It seems likely that during the first few years after his call and his marriage to Gomer he preached in the same spirit as that of Amos—being concerned with the demands for justice.

But Hosea's message was radically changed due to a tragedy within his family. After the birth of three children, he discovered that Gomer, his wife, was unfaithful to him. She may have left the faith of their household and taken up the religious claims and practices of the fertility religion of Asherah. The followers of this fertility religion, a hangover from the Canaanites and Phoenicians (especially through Jezebel), believed that fertility of the soil and of animals was dependent on sexual intercourse between Baal (the land god) and Asherah (his consort). In order to induce the Canaanite gods to productivity, men and women engaged in sexual intercourse to induce by imitative act the deities to similar activity. This was done in the name of religion. For that reason the Hebrew text of Hosea refers to such women as "holy ones." Gomer was a "holy woman" from the Canaanite point of view but a prostitute from Hosea's and our point of view.

As the months passed, Hosea realized that he loved Gomer, even though she had forsaken him for other men. Hosea diagnosed her trouble as being interested in the gifts of her lovers rather than in the lover himself. He prayed about his marital problems and believed that God wanted him to search for Gomer, find her, and bring her back to the household, reinstating her as mother of his family. So Hosea, who still loved her, sought for her and finally found her at a slave market, being sold as a common slave. He purchased her and restored her to her former position in the home. Out of this tragedy, Hosea learned that God too loved the sinner Israel. There is a divine love that never forsakes the object of that love. "O Love that wilt not let me go" is a man's perennial experience as he becomes aware of the presence of the loving Father.

So the book of Hosea was written not only to record his sermons but also to explain how he happened to change his message from the justice of God to the love of God. At first Hosea's central theme had been that of Amos: God desires not sacrifice but *justice*. Then, after his family tragedy with Gomer, his message became: God desires not sacrifice but steadfast love.

Hosea's book is concerned with spelling out what disloyalty (unfaithfulness) to God means. First, he points out that Israel brought gifts in order to obtain the gifts of grain and wine from God—they sought gifts, not God! They brought sacrifices, without loyalty (Hos. 6:6). Second, Hosea pointed out that unfaithfulness ("whoredom" to God) was engaged in when Israel practiced sacred prostitution in the gardens of the Canaanite fertility deities or violated the moral laws of the Ten Commandments (Hos. 4:1-2) or sought national security through other nations by sending embassies to Egypt or Assyria for security purposes.

Hosea was a revolutionary, too, as was Amos. Amos had dared to suggest that God was interested in all nations, not just Israel alone, and that what happened to his "elect" would be determined by their moral choices—for justice alone determined their future. Hosea taught the revolutionary concept that God desired not only a life of justice but a life of steadfast love (loyalty) to God. The ancient doctrine of election is thus given a fresh reinterpretation by Hosea, for the concept of the chosen people is now understood as demanding in return the nation's willful choice of a life of loyalty to God. No other thing, being, or nation is to be held in a superior place to Yahweh. Indeed, so strong is God's love and his election that if Israel strays, she will be chastised, and then reclaimed after she has been purged.

Needless to say, this book by Hosea greatly influenced not only later prophets, such as Isaiah and Jeremiah, but also the Apostle Paul and all Christendom.

Isaiah

The northern kingdom, Israel, was noted not only for her political, military, and economic astuteness but also for her prophets. From the northern kingdom came Elijah, Elisha, Micaiah, and Hosea. Amos, though a Judean, also preached in the northern kingdom.

After the northern kingdom was destroyed in 721 B.C., the southern kingdom assumed leadership in prophetic activities.

Isaiah was only a lad when Amos and Hosea voiced their prophecies in Bethel. Isaiah certainly knew their works, if not the prophets themselves. He lived through those same years which Amos and Hosea witnessed, when nationalism and economic pride made all Israel assume that she was specially blessed of God. The northern king, Jeroboam II, and the southern king, Uzziah, ruled for long reigns of forty years each. Prosperity inflated the egos of both nations. Both kings and people plainly placed their trust in embassies to various nations and in the might of their military power.

Isaiah was called to preach in 742 B.C. at the time of the death of his beloved king, Uzziah. Isaiah's ministry lasted over forty years, closing around 700 B.C. or a few years thereafter.

Before turning to his message we ought to look at the book of Isaiah as it now is. The book has sixty-six chapters. It is quite clear however that Isaiah, who prophesied in Jerusalem did not write the entire book. Isa. 40–55 is quite different from the first thirty-nine chapters of Isaiah. The first thirty-nine chapters deal with the period when Judah's kings were Jothan, Ahaz, and Hezekiah; Isa. 40–55 deals with a period two centuries later, when Cyrus was preparing to capture Babylonia. The prophet called this Persian ruler, Cyrus, the "anointed" (messiah) of the Lord.

When Isa. 1–39 was written, Jerusalem was filled with

happiness, confidence, pomp, and prosperity, and the Temple was considered a symbol of hope. But when Isa. 40–55 was written, the people of Jerusalem were filled with despair, the city was in ruins, and the Temple had been destroyed by Nebuchadnezzar (in 587 B.C.). Furthermore, the theological ideas of the two sections (Isa. 1–39 and 40–55) are quite different, as are also the language and style. The early chapters emphasize the holiness of God and the greatness of the Davidic dynasty, while chs. 40–55 emphasize the "suffering servant," and God as creator-redeemer, speaking of a new exodus, a new covenant, and a "new thing" to be done by God.

By similar reasoning, scholars date Isa. 56–66 as having been written about 510 B.C. or 450 B.C. We must distinguish between the three (or more) prophets who wrote in these three periods of the history of Israel and whose works were united in the large scroll we know as Isaiah.[2]

Our concern at this point is with Isaiah of Jerusalem, who was called to be a prophet in 742 B.C. The record of his call is one of the great passages in religious literature (Isa. 6) for it describes carefully not only the psychological processes through which the divine encounter took place but also the theological insights which came from this encounter. For centuries religious literature, including our own great religious poetry, has been greatly influenced by the expressions of Isaiah's faith. From his

> "holy, holy, holy is the Lord of hosts;
> the whole earth is full of his glory (Is. 6:3)

comes our great hymn of praise: "Holy, Holy, Holy, Lord God Almighty."

In the spirit of Amos, Isaiah denounced the view that God was interested in the size or number of the gifts left at the altar; he upheld Amos' view that God wanted men to

---

[2] It seems likely that most of Isa. 56–66 is a compilation of the work of several men.

> learn to do good;
> seek justice,
>   correct oppression;
> defend the fatherless,
>   plead for the widow.
> (Isa. 1:17; compare with Amos 5:23-24)

In the spirit of Hosea, Isaiah upheld the relationship of steadfast love (loyalty) to God as the primary requisite for maintaining right relationships. He denounced King Ahaz on the grounds of distrust and disloyalty to God when he said:

> If you will not believe,
> surely you shall not be established (Isa. 7:9).

This same infidelity was pointed to by Isaiah when his king sent ambassadors to Egypt, Philistia, Syria, and other countries, seeking security in them (Isa. 18:1) rather than in God.

Isaiah considered his nation's trust in foreign alliances as a basic distrust in God. He called on his people to practice in national life what their lips said on the days of their great religious festivals! To those who, in Hosea's words (Hos. 7:11), flitted about like a silly dove in search of security, he pleaded: "In quietness and in trust shall be your strength" (Isa. 30:15).

Isaiah called his people to trust in God as the active, creative Spirit, the Lord of history, who is more effective than an army of charioteers (Isa. 31:1-3). Isaiah considered his nation's search for national security through military alliances with other nations, such as Egypt, a basic infidelity to God. Apparently Isaiah was influenced by Hosea who, having experienced Gomer's unfaithfulness, denounced infidelity as the key problem to man's relationship to God.

In reading the message of Isaiah, one should keep in mind the prophet's concept of infidelity as the basic sin of man. Infidelity showed itself in several ways, not only in the throne's search for security, but in every man's economic selfishness, greed, and lack of concern for the welfare of those in need.

Isaiah, differing from Amos and Hosea, did not ground his faith in Judah's glorious future in the great events of the Exodus or of the Sinai covenant. Isaiah looked to the Golden Age of the reign of David and Yahweh's covenant with David. Isaiah assumed that God had chosen David and his descendants, as well as his city, Jerusalem, as the media through which his purposes would be achieved. He argued, for example, that Jerusalem would not be destroyed in warfare, for was not the holy Temple in the city of Zion? It is not difficult to understand, then, that during the last years of his ministry, between the age of sixty-five or seventy, Isaiah dreamed of a time to come when some "anointed" (messiah) of David would rule from Zion over Judah. Such an "anointed" would be filled with truth, justice, and loyalty to God. From David's line would come one who would be called

> Wonderful Counselor, Mighty God,
> Everlasting Father, Prince of Peace (Isa. 9:6).[3]

Amos had taught that God sought justice from his creatures. Hosea had taught that God sought steadfast love, yet Isaiah, accepting both emphases, went a step further than both of his contemporaries by declaring that true religion was a steady, unquestioning, confident trust in God. It is this emphasis which influenced Habakkuk, who in turn influenced a Pharisee by the name of Saul of Tarsus. Saul's emphasis of this idea gave the world the doctrine of justification by faith. Isaiah's concept of faith, colored by Habakkuk and Paul, was to nourish Augustine, Luther, and Wesley.

---

[3] While many scholars date the messianic passages of Isa. 9 and 11 in the postexilic period, there is a marked trend to consider these passages as having come from Isaiah at the close of his long ministry.

Micah

Micah lived at Moresheth, southwest of Jerusalem. He was a contemporary of Hosea and Isaiah, according to the first verse of his book, which states that he lived during the reigns of Jotham, Ahaz, and Hezekiah about 742-687 B.C. It seems probable that most of his ministry was in the period when Sennacherib, the Assyrian, invaded Judah (701 B.C.).

Judah was invaded by the military forces of Assyria three or four times during Micah's lifetime. These forces "lived off the land," a fact which made it most difficult for those farmers who lived in the rich lowlands of Judah.

But in between the years of foraging Assyrian soldiers, the farmers of Judah, such as Micah of Moresheth, had to borrow money to purchase seed and equipment for farming. The farmers would hardly get their loans paid off before the invading Assyrian soldiers would come again. It seemed to Micah and his contemporaries that the money-lenders of the capital city were most unfair in their methods of lending money and foreclosing on property.

> They covet fields, and seize them;
>   and houses, and take them away;
> they oppress a man and his house,
>   a man and his inheritance (Mic. 2:2).

To Micah's countrymen it seemed that the rapacious rich

> tore the skin from off my people,
> and their flesh from off their bones (Mic. 3:2).

Micah declared, in the spirit of Amos, that God was against injustice, bribery, and those prophets whose sermonic content was determined by the size of the collections (Mic. 3:9-11). Micah was thus the prophet of the common people, championing their cause against the ill-motivated purposes of the city. Little wonder that in his book the hope for a new son of David would come from the country—from Bethlehem.

Micah is remembered mostly for the wonderful chapter six in which he defines religion in terms of the teachings of Amos, Hosea, and Isaiah. Micah asked the question: What does God want of man? He refuted several possible answers, such as bringing a year-old bullock for sacrifice or indeed "thousands of rams" or "ten thousands of rivers of oil" or even "my first-born . . . the fruit of my body for the sin of my soul." He concluded his argument with the great definition of true religion:

> And what does the LORD require of you
> but to do justice, and to love kindness [or steadfast love]
> and to walk humbly with your God.

Micah unites the insights of Amos (justice), Hosea (steadfast love or loyalty), and Isaiah (humble trust in God) in this passage. Little wonder that it has been called the "quintessence of religion."

CHAPTER 4

The Literature of Judah
in the Seventh Century B.C.

JUDAH'S MOST PAGAN king, Manasseh, ruled for forty-five years (687-642 B.C.). The son of the religious reformer, Hezekiah, Manasseh reversed his father's policies. In doing so, he likewise negated all the teachings of Isaiah, who had been the prophetic instigator of Hezekiah's reform.

During Manasseh's reign Assyria built the greatest empire in history—extending the borders as far south as Thebes in Egypt. Manasseh, king in a small country, paid fealty to the Assyrian monarchs. He apparently believed that the Assyrian deities were more effective than Yahweh, for he brought an Assyrian altar back to Jerusalem and placed it in the temple area, instituting the worship of "all the host of heaven" (sun, moon, and stars were considered deities). Moreover he reopened local pagan shrines in the villages bordering Jerusalem. In addition he joined the worship of Yahweh with that of Baal so that Yahweh was worshiped at the pagan Canaanite "altars of Baal"; and even worse, an Asherah (a symbol of the mother-goddess) was set up beside the altar, and sacred prostitution was encouraged (II Kings 21:1-9; 23:7).

Besides these idolatries and apostasies King Manasseh reinstated the practice of human sacrifice when he "burned his son as an offering" (II Kings 21:6). Tradition claims that when the prophet Isaiah denounced Manasseh's apostasy, the King ordered him to be put in a hollow log and to be sawn in half. Manasseh's rule brought Judah to a dark age of her history.

Against this dark night of the soul many loyal Judeans looked to the faith of their fathers. Since their king, who was

101

of the dynasty of David, had proved false and evil, they did not look to the Davidic covenant as the ground of their faith as Isaiah had done. They went back to the earlier periods, to that of the events through which God had saved his people at the Sea of Reeds, to his covenant at Sinai, to his gift of the Ten Commandments, and to his disciplinary providence during the forty years at Kadesh-barnea.

We might say they "rediscovered Moses." Those who wrote religious literature during this period looked to the past for their inspiration and for the ground of their hope. One writer expressed it this way: "Ask now of the days that are past" (Deut. 4:32). In pointing to the past, Jeremiah and the Deuteronomist looked beyond King David and the monarchy to the great days of the Exodus and Sinai.

The literature of this period includes: (a) the union of the J and E traditions; (b) the poems of Zephaniah; (c) the early poetry of Jeremiah; (d) Deuteronomy; (e) Jeremiah; (f) Nahum; and (g) Habakkuk.

The Union of the Two Histories

After the fall of the northern kingdom, of Israel in 721 B.C., some deeply concerned Israelite (probably a priest) kept the royal and priestly records of the kingdom. These eventually found their way into the hands of a broad-minded religious man of Judah. He felt that the northern records of God's providential care of Israel were worthy of being read by others and preserved for future study.

When the dark ages of Manasseh came upon Judah, a Judean, loyal to Yahweh, decided to unite the two traditions, the E-tradition (the historical records of Ephraim, that is, Israel) and the J-document (the historical records of Judah). This was done during the first half of the seventh century B.C. It seems probable that fragments of the E-tradition were inserted into the J-document. The combined records formed the basic source for our accounts of the patriarchs, the Exodus from Egypt, the saving events at the Reed Sea, the experiences at Sinai, and the sojourn at Kadesh-barnea. This union (referred to as JE) of the two basic histories of Ephraim (Israel) and Judah lifted up the great history of the past. By lifting up the faith of the fathers these writings contradicted the idolatries and apostasies of the reigning monarch, King Manasseh. It was a daring act of faith by the royal recorder. We wonder if his blood flowed on the city streets (see II Kings 21:16) for this brave stand in writing of Yahweh's saving acts in the life of the people. Perhaps his brave pen encouraged other persons, such as Zephaniah, Jeremiah, and possibly the Deuteronomist, to write their records.

Zephaniah

The prophet Zephaniah, a descendant of King Hezekiah, prophesied in the days when Josiah, though a youth between twelve and eighteen years of age, was king of Judah. His ministry was before the days of the Deuteronomic reform (621 B.C.) and perhaps included the years when Scythians were invading the Assyrian Empire. For these reasons we date Zephaniah's ministry sometime between 628 and 622 B.C.

Zephaniah, a son of royal descent, showed no interest in the conditions of the poor man. His interests were with the leaders (prophets, priests, and public officials), all of whom he condemned (Zeph. 3:3-4). Since he knew nothing of Deuteronomy, we must conclude that his denunciations of religious syncretism—worship of Baal, astral deities, and Milkom—grew out of his knowledge of the messages of Amos, Hosea, and Isaiah. It seems likely that he also knew the historical document JE which emphasized belief in one God and denounced all idolatry. Having appropriated this heritage of faith, Zephaniah denounced the apostasy of the royal family. He warned that King Manasseh's infidelity and paganism would bring disaster to the nation.

In the spirit of Amos and Isaiah Zephaniah declared
that the "Day of the Lord is at hand" (Zeph. 1:7, 14-16)
and it would be

> A day of wrath . . .
>   a day of distress and anguish,
>   a day of ruin and devastation,
>   a day of darkness and gloom,
>   a day of clouds and thick darkness,
>   a day of trumpet blast and battle cry" (Zeph. 1:15-16).

The purpose of the poet-prophet Zephaniah was to bring
change in the lives of his hearers. His purpose was not to
entertain, nor to denounce the leaders of his day, but to
bring men to a decision for God, to repent of evil, and to
renew their pledge of loyalty to God's covenant. Hence his
cry:

> Seek the Lord, all you humble of the land . . .
> seek righteousness, seek humility.
> (Zeph. 2:3; compare with Amos 5:14-15)

The Early Years of Jeremiah

Another prophetic voice, also from Jerusalem, though
not from the royal line, was Jeremiah. His call to prophecy
came in the same period as that of Zephaniah. He began
to prophesy in the thirteenth year of Josiah (626 B.C.)
and ministered to his people for over forty turbulent years.
Though we will study the major part of his work after
discussing the book of Deuteronomy, we need to observe
that the first few years of his ministry overlapped with
the ministry of Zephaniah.

Jeremiah came from a priestly family of Anathoth, a
village about three miles northeast of Jerusalem. Jeremiah's
early ministry was deeply influenced by Hosea, as his metaphors suggest: He speaks of God's love for his bride in the
wilderness, Israel as a faithless wife, her harlotry (in-

fidelity), her breaking of the marriage contract (covenant at Sinai), her need to learn to say "my father."

Jeremiah thus based his faith not on the covenant made with David and his descendants but on the covenant made with Israel at Sinai and Kadesh-barnea. Here he differed widely with Isaiah who highly honored the Davidic covenant, for living in the shadow of King Manasseh, he could find no hope in a son of David. He turned therefore to the events in the days of Moses for hope. He too "rediscovered Moses."

It was during this early ministry that Jeremiah preached the messages found in the first six chapters of the book of Jeremiah and possibly also Jer. 8:14-17 and 10:19-22. These sermons were preached in poetic form at Anathoth. His ministry at Jerusalem began after discovery of the book of Deuteronomy (621 B.C.). These early poems (sermons) of Jeremiah were written down by Jeremiah and his secretary twenty years after their first delivery. They were primarily concerned with his call, his declaration of Judah's infidelity, Judah's consequent breaking of the covenant, and Jeremiah's proclamation of the coming Scythian invasion as one of the events of history which was directed by the purposes of God—as a method of arousing Judah to repentance for infidelity. Behind this latter concept is that of Amos, Isaiah, JE, and Hosea that Yahweh is the Lord of history and that he is seeking in the political events of history to work out his purposes for mankind.

Deuteronomy

The literary masterpiece of this period is the book of Deuteronomy. Though "found" in Solomon's Temple in 621 B.C., it was written before that time, very likely during the reign of Judah's evil king, Manasseh. Most scholars agree that the basic scroll found by the scribe Shaphan is found in chs. 5-26, 28. This scroll was declared by the prophetess Huldah to be "the Word of God." Josiah gave state support to this declaration and thus the first book of scripture was canonized. Since it was the first book to be called the Word of God, it has great interest for us.[1]

The writer of Deuteronomy, facing the idolatry and paganism of Manasseh (with its worship of astral deities, its fertility gods and goddesses, child sacrifice, ancestor worship, and so forth), wrote this book to both refute Manasseh's apostasies and to affirm his belief in the faith of ancient Israel. The author of the book of Deuteronomy offered a fresh interpretation of the faith of the fathers for his contemporaries.

The book of Deuteronomy is basically an expansion of the ancient confessional creed expressed in Deut. 26:5-9. The emphasis is on God's saving acts in the historical events at the Exodus, at the Sea of Reeds, at Sinai, and at Kadesh-barnea.

Though the writer's perspective is backward ("Ask now of the days that are past"), his purpose is to help Judeans see that he who led them in the past would lead them in the present. To achieve this goal, the writer of Deuteronomy presented his material in the form of a farewell sermon by Moses, but Moses is pictured as speaking not to his (Moses') generation but to those of the writers' generation (about 650 B.C.): "Not with our fathers did the Lord make this covenant, but with *us*" (5:3, italics added). The attempt to make faith relevant for their day is evident.

A description of the "Deuteronomic reformation" as established by King Josiah is found in II Kings 22–23. It speaks to the paganism which Manasseh's reign ushered into Judah but goes further: It "outlaws" all local shrines throughout the land and centralizes worship in one place, "the place which Yahweh your God shall choose." Interestingly enough, it does not name the city where worship should be centralized. Some have thought that the earliest

---

[1] Some scholars suggest that Deuteronomy was written a century earlier in Israel (the northern kingdom) possibly at Shechem or Bethel during the ministry of Hosea and Isaiah.

writer might have been a northerner, and therefore he was thinking of Shechem (the location of Abraham's first altar in Canaan, and also the place where Joshua created the twelve-tribe confederacy, about 1220 B.C.). We do not know whether Shechem or Jerusalem was intended, but we do know that King Josiah was politically alert and that he made Jerusalem the religious capital. To this day Samaritans argue for Shechem!

The present book of Deuteronomy consists of three "Mosaic" sermons (chs. 1-4; 5-26 and 28; and 29-30), the "Shechem" ch. (27), and a concluding supplement concerning Moses' last instructions, his blessings, and death (chs. 31-34).

The writer artistically wove together the priestly concerns for ritual and festivals with the prophetic concerns for justice, loyalty, and love. He assumed that Amos' demand for justice would be fulfilled if the commandments of God were obeyed; Hosea's concern for the love of God would be fulfilled when hearts become grateful for God's mighty acts in the past; Isaiah's demand for trust and steadfast loyalty would find fulfillment when they refused the way that led to death and chose the way that led to life (Deut. 30:15-20).

Nahum

Nahum wrote in the years of Assyria's decline and fall. In 614 B.C. the great Assyrian city of Ashur fell to the Medes. The Medes had also attacked Nineveh that year, though they did not capture it. When Nabopolassar, king of Babylonia, joined Cyaxares, king of the Medes, their combined forces destroyed Nineveh (612 B.C.). Nahum's poem is an ode to the fall of the hated Nineveh.

To understand Nahum's hatred of Nineveh, and his excessive nationalism, we must recall how the Assyrian military forces had swept across Palestine for centuries. We noted how Micah had faced the ravaging military forces of Assyria four times in his lifetime. The soldiers took food and anything else they wanted. They took their booty home with them. Nineveh, therefore, was noted for its wealth and splendor, obtained from other nations during the centuries. The conquered countries were decimated of their populations, their lands plundered, their women raped, their crops destroyed or stolen.

Little wonder that the poet, Nahum, could gloat over the fall of Nineveh. He wrote during the period when the Medes and Babylonians were devastating the land of the Assyrians. Many nations applauded, even though they themselves would feel the iron fist of Babylon within a few years. Nahum pictured the attack and conquest of the great Mistress of the World, Nineveh. The vividness of his description is unexcelled in Hebrew poetry: One can "see" his verbal picture of the furious drive of the cavalry and chariotry, the quick commands of officers, the capture of the proud queen and her ladies, the doom of Nineveh (Nah. 2).

This poem is the outgrowth not only of nationalism but of faith. Nahum clearly based his theology on the belief that Yahweh was the Lord of history as well as the God of justice. He was convinced that "the wages of sin [are] death." And this confidence came from the awareness that within the events of history was the creative spirit of God whose demand for justice from all nations applied equally to Assyria as to Israel and Judah. Nahum's weakness lies in the fact that he did not discover Hosea's emphasis that God is also the God of love. Nahum's poem, therefore, is theologically out of balance; but from a literary point of view his work rates among the best poetry of ancient Israel.

Habakkuk

Millions of Christians have begun their worship services with Habakkuk's call to worship:

> The Lord is in his holy temple;
> let all the earth keep silence before him (Hab. 2:20).

Habakkuk, who wrote about 600 B.C., is one of the unknowns of the prophets. His book is composed of three different literary forms: (a) a dialogue (Hab. 1:2–2:5); (b) a prophetic poem of five woes (Hab. 2:6-20); (c) a hymn (Hab. 3:1-19) taken from the ancient psalter, possibly around 300 B.C.

The theme of all three literary forms deals with the question of the nature of God and the problem of suffering. Habakkuk announced that the Chaldeans, a rapacious, unjust, yet victorious people, were to be used as the "rod of the Lord" against Judah (Hab. 1:6). How, he asked, could God reconcile his actions (of using evil nations) with his good nature? The answer to his questions is simply: Judgment will come on evil nations; God's purposes may seem to be slow in fulfillment, yet they will be fulfilled; those who are loyal to God, even though they suffer, shall live by their faith. Habakkuk's greatest and most influential statement was, "The righteous shall live by his faith" (Hab. 2:4). The apostle Paul, Augustine, Luther, Wesley, Barth, and countless millions have found a rebirth of spiritual life through recognizing the validity of this claim.

Jeremiah

We have noted previously (see "The Early Ministry of Jeremiah") that Jeremiah was called in 628 B.C. and that he preached in his home village of Anathoth until the Deuteronomic Reform was introduced in 621 B.C. After 621 B.C. he preached in several cities. It seems probable that Jeremiah upheld the reformation and preached its message, urging his fellow citizens to support it.

In urging his fellow citizens of Anathoth to support the Deuteronomic Reform, Jeremiah was urging them to destroy their ancient shrines, to cease and desist from offering sacrifices and offerings and from observing pilgrimages and annual festivals. With the closing of the shrines his own priestly family became unemployed too. Needless to say, the villagers (and perhaps even members of his own family) tried to kill him (Jer. 11:21).

The famous "Temple address" (Jer. 7) came shortly after the death of King Josiah, who had tried to keep Pharaoh Neco at Megiddo from going to the aid of the Assyrian forces in the north. Judeans, in extreme national-istic fervor, put Josiah's son, Jehoahaz, on the throne, but he was sent to Egypt in chains by Neco (II Kings 23:33-34). Neco then put Jehoiakim, another of Josiah's sons, on the throne. With increased religious fervor, Judeans centralized worship in Jerusalem and outlawed all paganism, as re-quired by Deuteronomy. Judeans then assumed, because of their obedience to the requirements of Deuteronomy, that God would *reward* them for their obedience to the Law. Having outlawed all other shrines, they assumed that the Temple in Jerusalem, the symbol of God's presence in their national life, would assure them national safety. When Jeremiah denounced the religious depravity and hypocrisy of the people and prophesied the destruction of the Temple by Nebuchadnezzar, a frenzied mob almost lynched him (Jer. 7 and 26).

The popularity of the reform subsided when the masses finally realized that neither Josiah nor Jehoahaz had been saved from their terrible fate by their zeal for the Law. Encouraged by Jehoiakim, they returned to the pagan practices of Manasseh. False prophets such as Hananiah fanned the fires of patriotism by false promises of peace, and prosperity. They based these promises on the fact of the presence of Solomon's Temple in their midst. But in 598 B.C. Jehoiakim, refusing to pay his tribute to Nebuchadnezzar, felt the attack of the Babylonian forces on his capital city, Jerusalem. The king died during the attack, and his eighteen-year-old son, Jehoiachin, succeeded him. He had to face the conquering Babylonian king and the humiliation of deportation to Babylon (with ten thousand of his choice people), where he lived in exile for the rest of his long life.

The book of Jeremiah is divided into four parts: (a) the autobiographical material by Jeremiah (1–25); (b) the biography of Jeremiah (26–45), probably written by Baruch his secretary; (c) oracles denouncing foreign nations (46–51); (d) the historical appendix (52), taken from II Kings 24:18–25:21, 27-30.

Much of the first two parts is repetitious, such as the Temple address, which appears in chs. 7 and 26. Some is distinctive, as is the letter of encouragement to the exiles in Babylon (ch. 29). Another distinctive literary (as well as psychological) form are his "confessions," which appear in the autobiographical sections. Here is expressed his doubt, distress, and futility—in fact, he dared to question God, suggesting that God had deceived him (Jer. 15:18).

During the fateful years of 597-587 B.C., Jeremiah used various literary forms to awaken Judah to her danger— allegory (Jer. 24), sarcasm, and finally symbolic prophecy (Jer. 27–28), but to no avail.

In spite of Jeremiah's efforts, Judah brought the wrath of the Babylonians down upon herself again, but this time the sacred city and Temple were destroyed, stone by stone. Thousands more people were taken into captivity to Babylonia. Jeremiah, however, stayed with the "bad figs," the people of the land. Within a few years Gedaliah, their governor, was murdered. In fear, his murderers escaped to Egypt, forcing Jeremiah to go with them. Apparently, he died in that foreign land.

But Jeremiah had developed a new type of literature: a devotional literature, in which the human soul—shaken by doubts, tormented by fear and anguish, sometimes twisted by bitterness—found inner peace, poise, and joy in the confidence of the closeness of God. Many of the psalms followed his new literary form as found in his confessions. Some scholars have suggested that Jeremiah is the "father of true prayer," inasmuch as he lifted up the life of communion with God as the highest achievement in life.

Jeremiah shifted the emphasis of religion in his day from the nation to the individual, from external acts of worship to the inner life of the worshiper. With his emphasis on the attitude of mind, he was a precursor of Jesus. Jesus himself depended greatly on Jeremiah's insights when he identified himself with the "new covenant" (Jer. 31:31) not made on tablets of stone as at Sinai, but in the thinking ("hearts") of men. This new concept of personal religion, of "internalizing" the claims of religion, marks Jeremiah as one of the greatest of the prophets.

CHAPTER 5

The Literature of Judah
in the Period of the Exile

Twice, in 597 and 587 b.c., Judah felt the conquering might of the Babylonian military forces of Nebuchadnezzar. Thousands of Jews were transported to Babylonia, among whom were such outstanding priests as Ezekiel and the writer of Isa. 40–55. Many more Jews were left behind in the ruins of their capital city and devastated countryside, including Jeremiah and an author of Lamentations. After several decades, some of the exiles returned from Babylonia to Judah, among whom were Haggai and Zechariah. There were great minds at work in both the land of exile and in Judah, attempting to interpret the faith under the new conditions that prevailed.

The literature which these men produced in this period of the exile, both in the homeland (in Judah) and in Babylonia, is the concern of this chapter. We shall study them in their chronological order, as follows: Lamentations, Job, Ezekiel, the Deuteronomic edition of Genesis through Kings, and Second Isaiah.

The Book of Lamentations

The book of Lamentations consists of five poems, one corresponding to each of its five chapters, lamenting the destruction of Jerusalem in 587 b.c. It is unlikely that any of these came from the pen of the prophet Jeremiah. The

113

style and ideas of Lamentations are generally very different from those of Jeremiah. Our Bible has the inscription concerning Jeremiah as the author because the Septuagint (the Greek translation of the Old Testament) has this statement at the beginning of the book:

> And it came to pass, after Israel was led into captivity and Jerusalem laid waste, that Jeremiah sat weeping and lamented with this lamentation over Jerusalem, and said.

Who the author was we do not know. We do know that whoever wrote Lam. 2 and 4 must have been an eyewitness to the destruction of Jerusalem in 587 B.C. He must have known Ezekiel and probably wrote in Babylonia about 560 B.C. The vivid descriptions of the siege and the horrors of it could only have been recorded by an eyewitness. The verbal pictures are so vivid that the reader can almost see the elders of Israel sitting on the ground in silence with dust cast upon their heads as a sign of mourning. One can see the eyes of the Judeans, red from many tears, and feel the pain of mothers whose children cry, "I'm hungry," and ask, "Where is food?" Listening closely, one can hear the hissing and wagging of the heads of the conquerors and stand in unbelief at the once beautiful temple now in ruins.

From a literary point of view the first four poems are of interest because they are acrostic poems—that is, each stanza begins with a successive letter of the Hebrew alphabet, until all twenty-two letters have been used. The first four poems are generally considered to be dirges, mournful songs for the dead (whence the title of "lamentations"). They are written in accordance with the meter for a dirge with four beats (or accents) in the first line and three in the second. The last poem (Lam. 5) is a prayer, written a half century later (about 540 B.C.) asking God to consider the misery of the exiles and to grant them restoration.

Job

The writer of the book of Job, living sometime in the sixth century B.C. (about 580-540 B.C.), was the most learned writer of the Old Testament. He was a man of encyclopedic knowledge. He had by far the greatest vocabulary of any Hebrew writer. The tremendous variety of literary forms he uses credits him with being a literary genius: Some of his poems are lyric; some are didactic; others are sarcastic parodies of traditions (Job 21:7-21, 31-33). Others reflect his knowledge and use of wisdom literature. His knowledge of flora and fauna, of religion and philosophy, social and moral law, of the psychological depths of man, of Oriental writings (Egyptian, Babylonian, Sumerian, Canaanite, Edomite, and so forth) help us understand one writer's evaluation of the book of Job: "The greatest poem of ancient or modern times."

The book of Job is composed of both prose and poetry. The prose, or narrative section, is an ancient folktale which existed before the time of David and Solomon (Job 1-2, the prologue; and 42:7-17, the epilogue). The main part of the book is in poetic form and lies between these two ancient prose sections.

The poet's work (Job 3–41) was carefully arranged: First he presented Job's lament (ch. 3); then the three cycles of dialogues between Job and his three friends (chs. 4–14, 15–21; 22–27); followed by Job's monologues (chs. 29–31). Then Yahweh answered Job out of the whirlwind, and Job repented (38:1–42:6). The third cycle was "corrected" by a later poet who sought to reestablish the orthodox view of Judaism by inserting ch. 28. Somewhat as an "afterthought" a later writer also inserted the speeches of Elihu (Job 32–37).

The theme which the poet has set forth in Job has been interpreted in two ways. Traditionally it has been argued that the poet discussed the problem of why a good man suffers, and why God, who is both absolute goodness and

absolute power, permits it. Another, more recent interpretation suggests that the problem of suffering is only
the occasion for probing a much more significant and deeper
problem. This second interpretation suggests that primarily
Job was searching for the meaning of life which he found
in his relationship to God.

The book proclaims religious heresy, thoroughly disagreeing with the theological orthodoxy of that day that
a man's religious condition could be evaluated by observing the blessings of possessions, children, and physical
goods which God had bestowed on him. The author of
Job denied the doctrine of rewards and punishment. The
meaning of life was not to be evaluated by adding up the
"gifts of God" but was to be determined by a man's personal relationship to God.

Though the problem of suffering is left unanswered in
this book, the problem of the meaning of human life is
found in faith (trust) in God as the Creator, in the recognition of the "creaturehood" of man, and in the necessity
of repentance.

The book of Job is thus more than the usual illustration
of wisdom literature. It reaches the prophetic dimensions
of man's concern for a life that finds meaning through
right relationships with the living God, the creator and
sustainer of life.

Ezekiel

Ezekiel's ministry extended from 593 to 571 B.C. He had
been one of the elite of Judah who had been taken into
captivity by Nebuchadnezzar in 597 B.C.

Ezekiel scattered fourteen dates throughout his book,
so that we have for the most part exact chronological information. The fall of Jerusalem in 587 B.C. divided
Ezekiel's ministry into two distinct periods. The first period
of his ministry (593-587 B.C.) was addressed to the people
back in Judah; the second period was addressed to the

Jews in exile in Babylonia. His call to prophecy came while he was in Babylonia (593 B.C.) possibly during a sandstorm (Ezek. 1:4). His religious experience was such that he became aware of the transcendence, the otherness, of God. In trying to define the nonphysical God, Ezekiel described him as being like light (Ezek. 1:4, 26-27), yet "seated above the likeness of a throne was a likeness as it were of a human form." His experience of God was real, yet ineffable: God had some affinities to humanity, yet was much more. The great, powerful, light-giving, personal God called him to preach to the house of Israel—that is, to the "household" in Judah. These sermons of warning and judgment are found in chs. 1-24. In these chapters Ezekiel used many devices—sermons, symbolic prophesying (Ezek. 4, 5), allegories (Ezek. 15-17), and even the death of his beloved wife—as means of communicating his anxiety. He was called to be a "watchman" like those on the city walls who called to the populace when enemies appeared. As a watchman Ezekiel called of coming catastrophe due to the vicious enemy within. He recognized immorality, bad religion, and especially infidelity (military alliances instead of faith in God for their security) as the real enemy of his country. History upheld his judgment, for Jerusalem was conquered in 587 B.C. The city was sacked, the Temple was completely destroyed, and for the second time thousands were taken into captivity to Babylon.

The second phase of Ezekiel's ministry began with the destruction of Jerusalem. In Babylonia he ministered to the exiles (585-571 B.C.). The records of this ministry are found in chs. 25-48.

Ezekiel's message to the exiles differed from the message he preached in Judah prior to the destruction of Jerusalem. He had preached doom to Judah, but now he preached hope and assurance. In the famous vision of hope in ch. 37—the vision of "the valley of dry bones"—Ezekiel assured the exiles that God willed that his people should live. The exiles, as in the days of slavery in Egypt, could respond to the Spirit of God. When that happened the ancient covenant would be renewed and the original promise would prevail: I will be their God, and they shall be my people.

Two of the great literary passages which greatly influenced the future were: (1) the image of the shepherd who lovingly cared for his flock and sought those who had strayed away (Ezek. 34:11-13; compare with Isa. 40:11 and Luke 15:3-7); and (2) the concept of a new spirit which God would give to his people: "A new heart I will give you, and a new spirit I will put within you; and I will take out of your flesh the heart of stone and give you a heart of flesh" (Ezek. 36:26). The influence of Jer. 31:31-34 seems evident here, with Jeremiah's concept of a new covenant, not on tablets of stone but within the heart of persons.

Ezekiel 40–48 gives assurance that God, who forsook Solomon's Temple in Jerusalem (in 586 B.C.) because of the immorality and infidelity of the people, would return and dwell with them. The prophet envisioned a new Jerusalem and a new temple in which God would tabernacle with his people. The temple would be the center of all activities, social, economic, and political as well as religious. The new community would be the covenant community, not the political. It would be similar to what Christians know as the *church*.

Expansion of the Historical Document

During the period of the exile the great national epic (JE) was expanded. We have previously observed how the two independent traditions, the J-tradition from Judah, and the E-tradition from Ephraim (Israel), were united during the first half of the seventh century B.C. in what we call JE.

Shortly after Deuteronomy was accepted as holy scripture (621 B.C.), a deeply religious writer wrote the books of I and II Kings (about 600 B.C.). His method was to choose material from the chronicles of the Kings (probably taken from JE) which illustrated the teachings of Deuteronomy, namely, that God would punish the nation for its religious infidelity. Since Deuteronomy called for the centralization of worship in Jerusalem, every king was judged by whether he did or did not permit worship to be practiced in "high places" other than in Jerusalem. All the kings of the northern kingdom were condemned, because they followed in the footsteps of Jeroboam II, who initiated and encouraged the worship of Yahweh not at Jerusalem but at Dan and Bethel. Likewise, all kings of Judah who permitted worship at shrines other than in Jerusalem or who worshiped other gods or permitted such practices in Jerusalem were condemned. Hezekiah and Josiah were especially lauded as good kings because of their religious reforms. King Solomon was condemned for his apostasy, for he permitted his wives, who, of course encouraged others, to worship their foreign gods in Jerusalem.

During the years of exile in Babylon, about 550 B.C., some very religious exiles decided to bring up to date the national epic which preceded the days of the kings. So the accounts of the period of Joshua, the judges, and Samuel (from JE) were reedited in the light of the teachings of Deuteronomy. The judges were evaluated by the same tests as that applied to the kings—whether they served other gods or were loyal to Yahweh only. This Deuteronomic evaluation may be stated in terms of a fourfold philosophy of history: (a) Israel sinned (was disloyal to God); (b) she was punished (plundered by the enemy); (c) she repented for her disloyalty, the cause of her punishment; (d) Yahweh sent a savior, a judge. This philosophy is clearly seen in Judges 2:11-19.

With this expansion of the earlier historical epic (JE) the literary situation was this: the book of Deuteronomy had been inserted into the original historical document (JE) just before the account of the death of Moses; then the book of Kings was edited in the light of the teachings of Deuteronomy (600 B.C.) ; and, finally, the rest of the historical books, which we know as Joshua, Judges, Samuel, Kings, were edited 550 B.C. Besides this expansion, which scholars refer to as JED (J-tradition, plus E-tradition, plus Deuteronomy), there were the prophetic books we have already discussed, such as Amos, Hosea, Isaiah, and others.

Second Isaiah

In our study of Isaiah of Jerusalem we observed that chs. 40–55 were written by another prophet. Since his name is unknown, scholars refer to him as Second Isaiah. Perhaps we could call him Isaiah of Babylon, since he was an exile in Babylonia and knew this capital city and its customs quite well.

This unknown writer of Isa. 40–55 surpassed all other writers of the Old Testament in his influence on Christian theology. His emphasis on God as the sole creator; man as a creature of God; God as judge and redeemer; the concept of the suffering servant who can save mankind through his vicarious suffering; the concept of hope— the coming of God's kingdom on earth; the faith that the time will come when every knee shall bend before Yahweh, and every tongue shall swear in his name (Isa. 45:23-24) ; the concept of the "light of the world" which would illuminate the way for all Gentiles—these expressions of faith made our unknown prophet a precursor of the Christ.

The poet of Isa. 40–55 was not only a prophet but also a great theologian. He differed from other prophets at the time of his messages: His message was never pessimistic; rather, it was optimistic. He did not call his contemporaries to repentance but assumed their repentance for the sins which forced Yahweh to bring the conquering Babylonians upon them. His writing was not presented in logical formation; rather, his thought was expressed in scores of brief poetic rhapsodies—poems of ecstacy as he thought of the nature of Israel's God and what he purposed to do for Israel and mankind.

Second Isaiah was steeped in the ancient faith of Israel. He called the people to sense the meaning of history: "Look to the rock from which you were hewn" (Isa. 51:1-2). He called them to renew their faith in God—not merely the God of their creed, but the living God. Yahweh had heard the cry of the oppressed slaves in Egypt; he had delivered them from their captors at the Sea of Reeds, making a highway through the waters for their journey; Yahweh had provided for their needs in the wilderness leading to Sinai and from Sinai to Kadesh-barnea; Yahweh had provided the Ten Commandments for their national life; and he had given them the land of Canaan. Since Yahweh was not merely the God of their creeds, but the living God, therefore, he heard their cry in their new slavery. He would deliver them from Babylon and provide a highway across the desert, even as he had provided a way across the sea (Isa. 40:3-5). Yahweh "purposed" to do a "new thing" for his exiled people: a "new" Exodus, a "new"' deliverance, a "new" highway, a "new" covenant (based on Hos. 2:16-20, Jer. 31:31-34, and Ezek. 36:25-26). Hence Second Isaiah called for a new song: "Sing to the Lord a new song" (Isa. 42:10). His poems urged the exiles to prepare for a new journey, for they were to return to the hills of Zion.

One of the glories of this poet-prophet-theologian is his sense of mission. Judeans were to return from exile, thanks to God's "anointing" of Cyrus (Isa. 45:1), in order that all mankind could learn to know God. The purpose of the return was not pure nationalism. Rather it was that the suffering servant (Isa. 53) should become the medium through whom God's being and purposes would be made known. Every exile, because of gratitude for his return through God's love and grace, was expected to become a priest to those who did not know God! Every ear was to hear Yahweh, every knee was to bend before him, and every tongue was to sing his praises. The dark places were to be made light, the uncertain places were to be made plain, because the "light" had now been brought to the Gentile world (Isa. 49:6b).

Isaiah-of-Babylon developed a new attitude, a fresh hope, a new guideline for Israelite thinking with regard to Yahweh and his activity. His expectations of a new Exodus, a new covenant, a new Israel, a "new thing" were fulfilled—though in ways he himself did not expect. For Christians the new covenant came into being with Jesus; the "new Israel" was born at Pentecost.

CHAPTER 6

The Literature of Judah
in the Persian and Greek Periods

After the Persian Cyrus the Great had conquered Babylon, he established a policy which permitted captives of war to return to their native lands. He also permitted them to take home the images of their deities and religious paraphernalia which the Babylonians had captured. He gave the exiles the right to redevelop their homelands, restore their temples, and reinstate their rituals. Cyrus considered himself the patron of all gods, which included of course Yahweh (Ezra 1:1-2).

In 538 B.C. Cyrus permitted the Judean exiles and other nationals to return to their native lands. He appointed Sheshbazzar, the son of King Jehoiachin the exiled king, to lead the Jewish exiles in making their return to Judah. Darius I appointed Zerubbabel, a descendant of King Jehoiachin, as successor to Sheshbazzar. Under the prophetic instigation of Haggai and Zechariah, the Temple was rebuilt in 516 B.C.

Additional exiles returned under the leadership of Nehemiah in 444 B.C. and under Ezra around 400 B.C. The literature of this Persian period comes during the leadership of these men: Haggai and Zechariah, Nehemiah, Ezra, and the author of the historical document of Chronicles. It seems likely that Third Isaiah (Isa. 56–66) was written in this period too, about 450 B.C.

Haggai and Zechariah

The great dreams of Second Isaiah were not fulfilled—there was no great exodus from Babylon, no great highways, no great sense of mission by the returnees in behalf of the Gentile world. It was not until the second return (520 B.C.) under Zerubbabel, that the Temple was rebuilt, and then it was only a small and inglorious structure in comparison to its former beauty. It lacked the splendor of Solomon's Temple, which had been produced by Phoenician architects and sculptors. When the old men who returned from exile saw the new temple, they wept with a loud voice (Ezra 3:12-13).

Haggai's four oracles were written in the year 520 B.C. Zech. 1–8 was written in 520-518 B.C. Chs. 9–14 of Zechariah are anonymous prophecies and were written much later. Both Haggai and Zechariah were responsible for the rebuilding of the temple, which was completed in 516 B.C.

Both prophets announced that Zerubbabel was the "anointed" and that Joshua, the high priest, would sit next to him on the throne. Together, the "branch" of David and the high priest would rule in justice and maintain Judah as a holy nation. Both prophets foretold a wonderful future for Judah and its Temple. They denounced the lethargy which permitted the Judeans to live in paneled houses, while the Temple lay in ruins. They promised a great economic future if the populace would arise and build the Temple. Their interests were Temple-centered, so sin was denounced in terms of rituals and festivals. Thus, one of the greatest sins of the people was in not keeping the Sabbath day according to the Laws of Moses.

Zechariah's oracles were cast in a literary style we call "apocalypse," which we shall study more carefully as it appears in the book of Daniel. Zechariah's prophecy abounds in cryptic language, weird visions of days yet to be, and of God's destruction of Judah's enemies with the establishment of his kingdom.

irreverence for God, unconcerned priests, disheartened and doubting worshipers, and the search for physical blessings in return for worship laid the foundation for the work of the great reformers, Nehemiah, and Ezra, as well as for the writer of the Priestly Code.

Of special interest is Malachi's use of the dialogical method. Instead of delivering prophetic oracles, he raised questions in order to start thinking and discussion. His discussion of whether God loved them or not (Mal. 1:2-14), the ideal priest (Mal. 2:5-7), the fatherhood of God over Israel (Mal. 2:10), and the blessings of obedience (Mal. 3:10-12, 16-17; 4:2-3) were most provocative.

Chronicles

The book of Chronicles originally included the books of Ezra and Nehemiah. When separated, Chronicles was divided into First and Second Chronicles, Ezra, and Nehemiah. The same person wrote First and Second Chronicles and Ezra and Nehemiah about 400 B.C.

The book of Chronicles is not so much "pure history" as it is an interpretation of Israel's history from a particular point of view. The sources used by the writer, the Chronicler, were mainly the books of Samuel and Kings. From these sources he selected, omitted, added, or modified according to his needs. He idealized David, presenting him not as he actually was but as the Chronicler thought he ought to have been. Thus David's years as an outlaw, his relationship with Bathsheba, and the palace rebellion by his son Absalom are not included in Chronicles.

The primary interest of the Chronicler was to present David as the real founder of the Temple, formulator of its ritual, and organizer of its staff of priests, Levites, musicians, custodians, and so forth. The book of Chronicles begins with David and ends with the fall of Jerusalem and its Temple in 587 B.C. Ezra and Nehemiah continue the account down to 400 B.C. with the giving of the Law by Ezra.

In reading First and Second Chronicles the reader must always keep in mind that the writer is *reinterpreting* Israel's history. He was presenting Israel, no longer ruled by kings, but by priests, in terms of "a kingdom of priests and a holy nation"—a people whose center was the Temple and whose acts of worship were cultic. The Chronicler was reinterpreting the history of his people so that they could see that his concerns for the Temple and its ritual were given by Yahweh at the time he made his covenant with David. The religious rituals and rites and customs of 400 B.C. were thus "frozen" by tradition, being grounded in the Golden Age of David, the founder of the cult.

Nehemiah and Ezra

Using some memoirs of Nehemiah and Ezra, genealogies, and other documents, the Chronicler continued his history of Judah from the fall of Jerusalem (587 B.C.) and the exile down to the giving of the Law by Ezra (around 400 B.C.). The continuation of this historical account is found in the books of Nehemiah and Ezra. These books tell about four different returns which the exiles made from Babylon to Judah; (*a*) the return under Sheshbazzar (around 536 B.C.); (*b*) the return under Zerubbabel and his rebuilding of the Temple (516 B.C.); (*c*) the return under Nehemiah (444 B.C.); and (*d*) under Ezra (about 400 B.C.)

Religion among those who stayed in Palestine was at a low point, as we noted from Malachi, but it was enthusiastically practiced by those who lived in exile in Babylonia. The exiles meticulously studied the Law of Moses; observed dietary laws, circumcision, and the Sabbath, and vicariously kept the festivals through reading their scriptures and rituals. So their faith was strong and the traditions were deeply imbedded.

When Nehemiah (about 444 B.C.) heard of the bad conditions which prevailed in Jerusalem, he asked permission from the Persian king, Artaxerxes I, for whom he was the cupbearer,[1] to return to his homeland with authority to make needed reforms. Permission was granted, and with royal authority for reforms, he returned to Zion and rebuilt the city walls of Jerusalem, denounced all marriages made with Gentiles, and established laws to assure purity of worship. His work was not very successful, however, for on his second trip (432 B.C.) he had to reinstitute his reforms.

Ezra was a priest in Babylon during the reign of Artaxerxes II (404-358 B.C.). He too heard of the bad religious, social, domestic, and economic conditions in Judah; therefore he decided to return. With papers from his king making him a state secretary for religious affairs, Ezra returned to Judah about 397 B.C. He too established rules for social and religious purity. He ordered that all marriages made with Gentiles be voided. But he had a better basis for requiring obedience, namely: he brought with him a codification of Mosaic Law.

There have been many suggestions as to what codification of laws Ezra brought with him from Babylon. These suggestions have included the Holiness Code (Lev. 17–26), the Priestly Code, Ezekiel's plans for the future (Ezek. 40–48), Deuteronomy, and the Pentateuch. The author of this book suggests the latter, the Pentateuch.

If the book from which Ezra read was the Pentateuch, then this was certainly a great contribution to the religion of the Jews. Ezra read before all Judah from "the book of the Law of Moses." This reading was concluded with a long prayer, a kind of confession of faith in which the basic elements of the old confessional creed of Shechem (Deut. 26:1-11) was recited, followed by confessions of sin, by repentance, and renewal of the covenant (Neh. 9).

----

[1] The position of "cupbearer" to the king was an office with great political importance. The king maintained an intimate relationship with his cupbearer, whose responsibility was to taste the king's wine and to act as guardian of the royal apartment. The cupbearer stood closer to the king than the bearer of the royal weapons. Nehemiah was the king's confidence man, his trusted friend.

Ezra may thus have given Judah its most prized possession, the Pentateuch, the first five books of the Old Testament, which was accepted as canonical shortly after 400 B.C.

With the acceptance of the Pentateuch, Judaism was
born. From that time forward, great emphasis was laid on
obedience to the Law of Moses. The Pentateuch expanded
the number of sacred scrolls from one (Deuteronomy) to
five: Genesis, Exodus, Leviticus, Numbers, Deuteronomy.

Ruth

The book of Ruth was written during the period when
Nehemiah and Ezra worked in Jerusalem. Its purpose was
to combat the teachings of exclusiveness by these two
leaders. They had argued that God's kingdom was to be
channeled through the blue bloods of Judah. Therefore,
Nehemiah had denounced mixed marriages, and Ezra had
issued an order abolishing their legal status. Some men
welcomed the decree, but some refused to accept it. As a
means of denouncing the claim of exclusiveness, a Jew
wrote the story of Ruth. Ruth, a Moabite girl, married a
fine Jew named Boaz. From their son came the great King
David. Inasmuch as King David was the epitome of all
that was good, the story made a telling point—good offspring can come from mixed marriages. The claim that
good can come from mixed marriages was a revolutionary
thought in the days following the social reforms of Nehemiah and Ezra.

The Priestly Code

In the fifth century B.C. some learned priests who had
remained with other exiles in Babylonia developed the
"Charter of Judaism," otherwise known as the "Priestly
Code."

A century earlier Jeremiah had written a letter from
Jerusalem to the exiles in Babylonia. Among various con-

cerns was the matter of worship while in a foreign land. He advised the exiles that, though they were far removed from Zion, yet they could worship God, not through offering of sacrifices but through prayer "when you seek me with all your heart" (Jer. 29:12-13; compare with Deuteronomy 4:27, 29). It was also during these days of exile that some Judeans wrote various psalms which expressed their prayer life, such as Ps. 130, "Out of the depths I cry to thee, O Lord!"

From the exiles' interest in prayer life there eventually developed group meetings for collective prayers. These were probably held in various homes at first, as in the case of Ezekiel, who met with the elders for instruction in the religious traditions and for prayers. From this "gathering together" for prayer came the word "synagogue."

The exiles, searching their sacred scripture in the hope of finding meaning in their situation, recognized the fact that their condition of exile was similar to that of the fathers in bondage in Egypt. They had no human king in either period, for Yahweh was considered their king. The priests knew Ezekiel well and recalled how he had emphasized the importance of the Temple and its ritual and priestly office in developing a holy nation in the future. These priestly writers therefore wrote a constitution to the theocratic (not *political*) state, which we call the Priestly tradition, the Priestly writing or the "Priestly Code"—to which we referred above. The sovereign king was God, his people were the Jews, the sovereign land on which his people lived was the land of Canaan given to them by Yahweh, the laws of the land were revealed to Moses and to be interpreted and upheld by the priests, and the system of taxation which upheld the structure financially was the tithe.

In that day, questions were being raised as to the origins of the religious institutions, such as the Sabbath, circumcision, the Passover, and the Law. The priestly writers answered these questions by showing how these were given by God at the end of each of four dispensations (or eras) of human history. These eras mark the four major divisions of the priestly work, so we should note them carefully.

The first dispensation was from *Creation to Noah* (Gen. 1:1–2:4a; 5:1-28). This age covered human history from Adam to Noah. Man was to have dominion over the creatures of earth, but not over one another—only God, the Creator, was sovereign. The first Jewish religious institution, the observance of the Sabbath, was God-given as a memorial of God's resting on the seventh day after creation. This document also pointed out that the Jewish calendar of festival days was determined by the creation of the moon, which marked off festivals by the lunar system: seven days, twenty-eight days, week of weeks, year of jubilee (seventh year), and so forth.

The second era of human history was from *Noah to Abraham* (Gen. 9–11). After the flood Noah offered the first sacrifices to God. This marked the origin of the sacrificial system and the shedding of blood from all animals. God made a covenant with all human beings at this time, giving the sign of the rainbow as a symbol that he would not destroy mankind again.

The third era was from *Abraham to Moses* (Gen. 17–50; Exod. 1–2). At this time God made a covenant with Abraham and his descendants. The sign of the covenant of the chosen people was circumcision. A second important feature in this era was when Abraham purchased the cave of Machpelah where Sarah was buried. This payment was considered as earnest money for the future claim of the land of Canaan.

The fourth era was from *Moses through the conquest of Canaan* (found in Exodus, Numbers, Leviticus, and Deut. 32:48-52; 34:1-4, 7-9). In this era God made known his name, "Yahweh," for the first time; he instituted the Passover; he gave the Ten Commandments and some other laws at Sinai; he gave instructions concerning building the

Tabernacle; he instituted the Ark and the offices of the priests; and gave rules governing ritual worship.

Of course the fourth era was most important to the priestly writer (s). God *gave* his revelation to Israel. Israel could only receive it. Moses mediated the Law, which was the "given" of God to Israel, and required her to make a decision relative to it. Her choice was a matter of life and death, for refusal inevitably led to unholiness and destruction; acceptance led to holiness and acceptance by God, hence to life. The Law, however, was not considered as a burden to Israel but as a means of grace, for through it the Israelites knew that God was near.

The key to the Priestly Code is: "I am God Almighty [El Shaddai]; walk before me, and be blameless" (Gen. 17: 1). The blameless life was the holy life. From this demand came the emphasis on legalism, as later seen in Phariseeism. The goal was a good one, sincere and well conceived, for it included both priestly and prophetic concerns of life. It is unfortunate, however, that these priestly writers could not capture the heights of Second Isaiah in his conception of the suffering servant being sacrificed for all mankind. Such a thought was perhaps inconceivable to priests, who saw only lower animals as proper sacrificial offerings. Even so, the Priestly Code was a great theological contribution to Judaism and mankind. The beauty of the story of creation (Gen. 1) is hardly excelled, even by Job and Second Isaiah. The concepts of the sovereignty of God and the idea of holiness have been recaptured by theologians of all centuries.

Protestantism has incorporated the inspiring priestly benediction, found in Num. 6:24-26, into its worship service:

> The LORD (Yahweh) bless you and keep you:
> The LORD make his face to shine upon you,
>   and be gracious to you:
> The LORD lift up his countenance upon you,
>   and give you peace.

The Psalms

The book of Psalms is often referred to as "the hymn-book of the second Temple." A more accurate designation might be "the devotional book of the synagogue." It was during the postexilic period (after the return in 520 B.C. and the decades following) that the various books of psalms, plus smaller groups and individual psalms were gathered together into one volume. They were not considered canonical for centuries, yet they were used for devotional purposes. The one hundred fifty psalms in the psalter were accepted as canonical at the Council of Jamnia, about A.D. 90.

The Psalms represent poetic expressions of faith during nearly eight hundred years. The earliest ones may have come even a few decades before the time of David. Several may well have come from that "sweet singer of Israel"; some, even from Solomon. Others came from unknown poets who sang their faith during the centuries. The psalms were ascribed to many persons—to David, Heman, Asaph, Ethan, Jeduthun, and others. Many of these, probably, represented musical guilds and not individual composers. Our present psalter is a collection of five different hymnbooks of post-exilic origin: (a) Pss. 1–41; (b) Pss. 42–72; (c) Pss. 73–89; (d) Pss. 90–106; and (e) Pss. 107–150. Undoubtedly each collection was drawn up from many separate psalms that existed separately or in smaller groups.

The period of the Exile was especially productive of psalms—some in the spirit of Jeremiah's "confessions," filled with doubts and troubled hearts which finally found their peace in the presence of God (Pss. 3, 5–7, 13, 17, 22, and so forth). Others expressed their pain and travail as they wearily marched from Judah to Babylonia: "On the willows there [they] hung up [their] lyres" (Ps. 137), unable to sing unto the Lord in a foreign land. Some expressed praises to the God of nature (as Pss. 8, 19, 29, 104); or praises to God, the Lord of history (Pss. 46, 47, 110, 114); or related their love of the Law (Ps. 1); or joy as they made their pilgrimage to Jerusalem to worship (Pss. 121–134). Psalm 150 is an excellent psalm with which to conclude the psalter—its full orchestra and levitical choirs join in singing their own "hallelujah" chorus.

Psalmists representing many centuries voiced their faith in God and praised him through many types of poetry. Their poetry may be classified in many different ways, as the many fine scholarly volumes on the psalms illustrate. One approach would be to study the psalms in chronological order, from the times of the monarchy down to the middle of the Greek period (about 200 B.C.); another approach would be to study them by the specific concern of each psalm—the part it played in worship, in the enthronement of a king, or as an invective against enemies. Whichever way we may study the psalms, we will find them for the most part to be among the best devotional material available. In reading them we soon discover that our hearts have joined those voices of the centuries of faith in a fresh song of praise to our God.

Joel

Sometime between 400-350 B.C. the prophet Joel witnessed an invasion of locusts in Judah, followed by a devastating drought. Joel interpreted these experiences as evidences of the coming Judgment Day. He called on the priests, leaders, and people to assembly for repentance. This forms the first part of his prophecy.

The second division of Joel's prophecies deals with the future. Joel 2:28–3:21 pictures the outpouring of God's spirit on all flesh (compare with Peter's use of this prophecy on the day of Pentecost, Acts 2:14-36) and the final judgment over the heathen who are to be crushed.

Joel wrote at a time when apocalyptic literature was beginning to replace prophecy. Apocalyptic literature looked to the future—to judgment of evil and to a glorious future for those loyal to God. Apocalypse (as found in Joel 2:28–

3:21) used strange figures of speech and metaphors to carry its message. The writers of apocalyptic literature believed that the future was in the hands of God. Justice, truth, and goodness would ultimately win because God was the Lord of history, and his purposes would prevail.

Apocalyptic literature also is found in Zeph. 2:4-15: Isa. 34; Ezek. 38–39; Zech. 14.

Esther

The historical setting for the book of Esther is the reign of Xerxes (486-465 B.C.) though it probably was written toward the end of the Persian period, about 350 B.C., during a period of persecution. This period of anti-Semitism was possibly due to the Jewish custom of "separating themselves" from other peoples. This "separating oneself" (the root meaning of the Hebrew word from which we get the word "Pharisee") from Gentiles was accomplished by simply observing the Jewish rules concerning clean and unclean foods (refusing to eat pig, camel, and so forth), observing the Sabbath (refusing to work on Saturdays), observing the feast days (recalling the great events to mind and praising God for his redeeming actions in them), circumcising the male infants, and offering morning and evening prayers to Yahweh. The exiled Jews in Babylonia emphasized their rules, customs, and festivals—their "separateness"—more than those who stayed in Judah.

Probably using the kernel of an historical event, now unknown, the writer of Esther wrote an "historical novel" about a period of anti-Semitism, when Haman (the leader of the Semitic persecution) almost succeeded in wiping out the entire Jewish population by decree of the king. However, lovely Esther ("Hadassah," her Hebrew name) saved the day. Willing to risk her life for her people, she swayed the decision of the king who was her husband, in favor of her people, thereby reversing Haman's plans. In fact Haman was hung on the very scaffold planned for the Jews.

Mordecai, Esther's uncle and fellow schemer, became prime minister in Haman's place.

The book of Esther seeks to give the origin of an old festival not found in the Law, called the Feast of Purim. "Pur" means "lot"; purim means lots. On the day Haman had determined by lots (purim) for the destruction of the Jews, he himself was hanged. This symbolized for the Jews of succeeding centuries the claim that God was continuing to work out their salvation and would save them even in times of persecution. This hope led to a rejoicing, dancing, and drinking. To this day the Feast of Purim is one of rejoicing in the assurance that ultimately the Jewish faith will prevail. On the negative side we must note that nowhere in Esther is there a hint of the suffering servant of Second Isaiah or a sense of mission to be a "light for the Gentiles" or of other prophetic insights.

Though the writer of the book of Esther did not refer to God nor to ethical demands throughout the entire book, his writings presupposed the faith of Israel—that the God of history was and is working toward fulfilling his purposes, which the book envisioned as being to save his chosen people. This is the book's major limitation! It reflects the narrow nationalism, the racial and religious pride of the reforms of Nehemiah and Ezra. It does not come to the heights of Ruth and Jonah. We should recall, however, that Nehemiah and Ezra were concerned about the purity of their faith. Their strong measures were taken out of concern for the syncretism of faith which they saw in Judah. The book of Esther was written to encourage the household of faith (Judaism).

Proverbs

The book of Proverbs is an anthology of wise sayings, maxims, aphorisms, adages, and ancient wisdom. Though compiled in the fourth century B.C., its contents come from many centuries—from some of the teachings of Solomon, from various learned Egyptians of antiquity, as well as from contemporary wise men. Proverbs is a library, similar to Psalms, inasmuch as it is a collection of several booklets of wise sayings.

The proverbs may be divided into two basic groups: those assigned to Solomon and those to foreigners. In the first group are four distinct collections (booklets): chs. 1–9; 10:1–22:16; 22:17–24:22 and 24:23-34; 25–29. In the second group, those assigned to foreign writers, are chs. 30 ("the words of Agur"); 31:1-9 ("The words of Lemuel, king of Massa"); and 31:10-31 (an alphabetic poem concerning a good housewife).

Proverbs, as is most wisdom literature, is both secular and religious in content, though it emphasizes the secular. A theme running throughout Proverbs is "the fear of the Lord," by which is meant religion, a humble reverence before God. Thus religion, that is "the fear of the Lord," is the beginning of wisdom. Proverbs, however, says practically nothing about worship—either from the prophetic or priestly point of view, except in the neutral passages (Prov. 7:14; 17:1) or in the very mild, negative allusions to sacrifice (Prov. 15:8, 29; 28:9). Proverbs seems to be ignorant of Israel's past—the mighty acts of God in history—the historical calamities of her past (the exile), and of her glorious future. The emphasis is on pleasing God so one can be successful in life.

The book of Proverbs has been thought to be a text used in academies whose students were young men from the upper class of society. The proverbs instructed the students to be philanthropic, not to get drunk, to beware of lewd women, to find spiritual meaning in wealth, and to beware the perils of wealth and poverty. The students were taught that there are some things in life more valuable than riches: wisdom (Prov. 3:13-14; 8:11, 19; 16:16), justice (Prov. 16:8), religion (Prov. 15:16), a good name (Prov. 22:1). They were taught that there are two ways of life: not only the way of Deuteronomy which taught of the choice that led to life and death (in obedience to God or in disobedience) but also the right and wrong way of conduct. The right way included the way of knowledge (wisdom) while the other is characterized by ignorance and falsehood.

One of the major themes running throughout this anthology is the doctrine of retribution, that is, of rewards and punishment. A young man should learn to so live that his life will be rewarded. This is the "successful" way of living, so a youth should guide his life accordingly. Yet back of this apparent secular emphasis are the foundation principles of reverence for God. The successful man's life is undergirded by his faith in God.

Ecclesiastes

Besides Proverbs and Job a third outstanding example of wisdom literature in the Old Testament is Ecclesiastes. It gets its name from a Hebrew word *Koheleth,* which means "one who addresses an assembly." The author is described as a sage, a teacher, a skilled writer (Eccl. 12:9-10). He certainly did not share the faith of King Solomon, who must be eliminated as the writer. Inasmuch as he was not a *preacher* of faith, we might better call him a *professor.* The date of his writing is approximately 250-200 B.C. It reflects the influence of the Greeks who conquered Palestine in 332 B.C. under Alexander the Great. At times he showed knowledge of Stoicism, then, of Epicureanism. He shared the Greek's love for wisdom. The Professor searched for the meaning of life but was unsuccessful. He was very pessimistic in his conclusions. In fact, his work was hotly debated at the Council of Jamnia (A.D. 90) before it was canonized.

The Professor taught his students that life is brief, full of sorrow, and meaningless—meaningless because man's reason is unable to search out God's ways to find his plan and purposes for life. The conclusion was pessimistic: "Vanity of vanities," says the Professor, "vanity of vanities! All is vanity" (Eccl. 1:2; 12:8). His despair of life, if not hatred of it (Eccl. 2:17), reminds one of some modern non-Christian existentialists who express nausea when contemplating life.

Though he argued, as did the Greeks, that life is cyclic, and that "there is nothing new under the sun" (Eccl. 1:4-9), yet the Professor affirmed his Hebraic faith that everything is "in the hand of God" (Eccl. 9:1). God is so transcendent that man cannot conceive his purposes; therefore, the Professor's pessimism arose out of the hiddenness of the almighty, transcendent God. There is no immanence in the Professor's thought, so God is the unknowable, though omniscient, God of the universe. The difficulty is not that there is no thread that binds the centuries together, but that man cannot see the threads—he does not have God's vision! The verdict is futility!

The difficulty of the Professor was not in his reasoning powers, but in his refusal to accept the Hebraic claim that God revealed himself through the events of history—thus showing his concern, love, justice, and providential care. Revealed theology could have helped him at the point where natural theology failed. But we must not overlook the fact that behind his pessimism is a firm faith in the transcendent God who orders all things and whose purposes will prevail.

Jonah

With the reforms of Nehemiah and Ezra in the last half of the fifth century B.C., many of the Jews became proud of their ancestry and arrogant about their religion. Many assumed an arrogance after having "read" the newly canonized Pentateuch (400 B.C.) which gave the Judeans a constitution for their theocracy and the belief that God had chosen them from all the peoples of the world. Nehemiah and Ezra helped to create racial pride by denying Judean men the right to intermarry with Gentiles. The book of Ruth was written to correct this narrow bigotry based on race.

Besides racial pride, religious pride was rampant. The assumption of many was that God had chosen Israel because the Israelites were a superior people. So a writer, in the same spirit as the one who wrote the story of Ruth, decided to write a short story to offset religious pride. The result was the book of Jonah.

The writer centered his story around a prophet named Jonah, who had lived in the days of Jeroboam II (see II Kings 14:25). To show how God reacted to religious arrogance and pride, the writer developed a story about a prophet, Jonah, being called to preach to the hated Assyrians at their capital city, Nineveh. (Recall how Nahum gloated over the fall of Nineveh in 612 b.c.) Jonah refused to preach to the Assyrians, lest they be converted, so he went in the opposite direction, taking a ship to Tarshish. The story is well known. A storm arose; the sailors found by lot that Jonah was guilty and threw him into the sea. Immediately the storm abated. A fish swallowed Jonah, only to spit him up on shore three days later. Jonah was again called to preach to Nineveh, so he decided to go. His preaching was so successful that not only the people but also the animals were ordered to put on sackcloth and ashes for repentance. In despair, for Jonah had not thought his enemies would repent, he withdrew from Nineveh and sat down to wait for further development. A plant grew quickly over him, giving him shade, but then it died overnight. He felt sorry for it. Then Yahweh asked him why he was sorry that the plant had died; it was just a plant. If he pitied the death of a plant, how much more would Yahweh pity the death of his people, the Ninevites. He should, therefore, rejoice that men, even his enemies, had found God.

The purpose of the book of Jonah was to recall Judeans to the universal mission of Second Isaiah—God had chosen Israel and Judah that they might be a light to the Gentiles,

that every knee should bow before the Lord, and every
tongue confess that he was God. Religious pride and arrogance were sins. God repudiated them even as he repudiated racial pride in the book of Ruth.

Daniel

With the acceptance of Deuteronomy as canonical (621
B.C.), a new era was born. Increasingly men inquired of
the Book rather than the prophet as to the will of God.
During the Exile, scholars had carefully studied their religious scrolls, seeking insight into the meaning of their
plight. During this same period, some prophets, such as
Jeremiah, Ezekiel, and Second Isaiah, spoke in the old
prophetic style: "Thus saith the Lord." By the time of
Haggai and Zechariah prophecy had been narrowed to interests in Jerusalem and Judah, not to universal demands;
and by the time of Ezra, prophecy had ceased.

Prophecy developed a new mode of expression, a literary
form called Apocalypse. Its major interest was in the future
rather than the present. It dealt with a timetable concerning the end of time and the consummation of history. It
came into being in an age when men of faith felt that they,
as men, could do nothing; conditions were so bad that only
God could change things. So they wrote of "hidden
mysteries" (apocalypse) —events which only God would determine and God alone knew when they would come to
pass.

We see the beginning of this type of literature in such
writings as that found in Ezek. 38–39, Zech. 9–14, and Isa.
24–27, which were probably written during the last days
of the Persian period or in the early Greek period. In each
of these passages a new style of bizarre visions and weird
symbolism appeared. In the Ezekiel passage the new age is
preceded by a great war brought against Jerusalem by Gog
(using Gyges [="Gog"] of Lydia, who reigned about 670-
652 B.C., as a type or symbol of Judah's enemies). Yahweh

is pictured as intervening in this final battle of history, bringing victory over all Israel's enemies, and ushering in the kingdom of God. (In the apocalypse in the New Testament—the book of Revelation—this last great battle is to take place at Armageddon, the "hill" of Megiddo.)

Apocalyptic writers were greatly influenced by Persian religious thinking—especially Zoroastrian dualism, which affirmed the existence of God and his archenemy, Satan (a fallen angel) .[1] Apocalyptic literature borrowed this Persian concept of Satan at the head of the kingdom of evil. New religious terms were appropriated, such as god of light, sons of light, god of darkness, sons of darkness. Israel's warfare was now pictured as a celestial warfare between the forces of Satan and the forces of God, with the final outcome certain, for only God's purposes would prevail.

Zech. 9–14 used the same apocalyptic idiom by picturing the last great conflict with all the nations gathered together at Jerusalem for the final battle (see also Joel 3:9-11). Yahweh is pictured as overthrowing the evil forces and as being accepted as King over all the earth. The so-called "little apocalypse" of Isa. 24–27 also portrays the scene of the Last Judgment; a great cataclysmic event takes place:

> The earth is utterly broken,
>   the earth is rent asunder,
>   the earth is violently shaken.
> The earth staggers like a drunken man. (Isa. 24:19)

The evil angels are to be punished and thrown into a pit (Isa. 24:22) ; the moon and sun will be eclipsed, chaos will reign. In the midst of this chaos the righteous of Judah will be secure:

---

[1] The traditional Hebrew view of Satan is expressed in the book of Job, where Satan had a highly respected position in the heavenly court. Here, Satan was the highly honored prosecuting attorney. By contrast, in Persian religious thought, Satan was the leader of the cause of those who live in darkness. He is the antagonist of God, the epitome of evil. He is a divine being equal to Ahura-Mazda, god of light, though the leader of the forces of darkness and evil.

> Thou dost keep him in perfect peace,
> whose mind is stayed on thee,
> because he trusts in thee (Isa. 26:3).

Furthermore, God "will swallow up death for ever, and the Lord God will wipe away tears from all faces" (Isa. 25:8a). Those who have trusted in God shall be resurrected that they may participate in the new age.

The book of Daniel was written in an era when apocalypse was a major literary form for expressing one's faith in the ultimate victory of God and his purposes for his world. It was written with the use of weird symbols (such as a ten-horned beast, a huge statue made of gold, silver, lead, and a mixture of mud and potsherds). Each must be deciphered in terms of the political situation of the writer's day and in terms of his firm faith in God's ultimate victory.

The book of Daniel was written about 165 B.C., three years after Antiochus IV Ephiphanes had outlawed Judaism. (When Alexander the Great died, his kingdom was divided between his three generals. The descendents of two of these generals controlled Palestine "off and on" during the next two centuries. So the Seleucids and Ptolemies struggled over the land of Palestine for many decades.) Antiochus IV Epiphanes, a Seleucid, attempted to force Greek culture on the Palestinians by building amphitheaters and gymnasiums, by requiring a common language, the *koine* (common) Greek, and by instituting worship of Zeus and himself ("God Manifest"). He therefore ordered that all Sabbath observances be discontinued, all reading and possession of the Torah cease on penalty of death, that circumcising of male infants cease on penalty of death, and all observance of all dietary laws cease. The governor sacrificed swine on the altar of burnt offerings in Jerusalem and desecrated the Temple in other ways.

Needless to say there were some who refused to obey this edict. A group of Hasidim ("pious ones") from Modein refused to eat the flesh of pigs and killed a Syrian officer who tried to order them to do so. Thus began the Maccabean revolt which resulted in Jewish independence lasting a century (165-63 B.C.).

The first six chapters of the book of Daniel are stories about how loyalty to God—as expressed in reading the scriptures, prayer, obedience to dietary laws—will be upheld by God himself. The flames of the fiery furnace and the mouths of hungry lions are under the control of Yahweh, Lord of creation as well as history. God will surely not permit evil to befall his loyal ones. "But if not, be it known to you, O king, that we will not serve your gods or worship the golden image which you have set up" (Dan. 3:17-18).

The second section of Daniel (chs. 7–14) uses the apocalyptic idiom. It consists of four visions which declare that the tyrannical rule of evil men will be brought to nothing and that God's kingdom shall be established on earth. The visions deal with the four successive empires of the Jews' postexilic experience—that is, with Babylonia, Media, Persia, and Greece. The Greek empire will be wiped out completely, but the other three will be ruled by "the saints of the Most High" (Israel) through God's intervention in their behalf. The two-horned ram of ch. 8 refers to the Median-Persian empire; the he-goat with a huge horn between his eyes (Alexander the Great) fought with the two-horned ram till the great horn broke but was replaced with four horns (Alexander's empire was divided into four parts). One of the four horns sprouted a "little horn" (Antiochus Epiphanes) who thought himself to be god—exalting himself above the heavenly host, defiling the Temple, and proscribing Judaism. "No human hand" would correct this state of affairs. Three years and two months after Antiochus Epiphanes outlawed Judaism, the Temple was rededicated (December of 165 B.C.) and services resumed. To this day the rededication is memorialized through the Feast of Lights (Hanukkah).

The remaining chapters of Daniel deal with the vicissi-
tudes of the Seleucid rulers. Jewish suffering through persecution was viewed against the background of God's purposes and thus was endured with poise.

Apocalyptic literature called for patience and loyalty to
the Torah at all costs; it called for faith that God's kingdom
would come. In contrast to the kingdoms of this world
God's kingdom would be from everlasting to everlasting.
These "tracts for bad times" helped countless thousands
to maintain their faith and loyalty to God even unto death.

Song of Songs

The title of this book states that this "Song" is the love-
liest of the 1,005 Solomon wrote (I Kings 4:32). "Song of
Songs" is the Hebrew way of saying it is superlative, just as
Holy of Holies means holiest.

For centuries, scholars have maintained that Solomon
did not write these love songs. These twenty or more poems
form an anthology of love lyrics and related poems. Some
may have been sung at weddings (as Song of S. 3:6-11, a
description of a wedding procession) or possibly sung in
honor of the bride as she danced before the wedding guests
(Song of S. 6:13–7:5). But for the most part the poems
are charming love songs which describe the lover's attitude
toward his beloved in the springtime.

The songs teach no lesson, nor do they tell a story. They
simply extol human love in courtship and marriage. God is
not referred to in any of the songs, so we should not seek to
find insights concerning his nature, will, or purposes. We
should take the songs as they are—love songs taken from
human experiences of love without reference to divine
love whatsoever. This does not mean, however, that the
writers, or singers of these songs were godless people. It
means that men of faith (including those who accepted
the Song of Songs as canonical) do sometimes sing songs
other than religious hymns.

During the past centuries, these songs have been interpreted in several ways: (a) *the allegorical,* in which the lover is Yahweh and the beloved is Israel; or the lover is Christ and the beloved is his church (John 3:29; Eph. 5: 22-33; Rev. 18:23; 21:2, 9); (b) *the dramatic,* in which the song is considered a drama with two characters, Solomon and the Shunammite (Abishag); or sometimes three characters, Solomon and the two lovers, a shepherd and the Shunammite who retains her love in spite of royal designs for her love; (c) the *liturgical* or cultic, in which the songs are seen as songs coming from ancient fertility rituals, adapted through the centuries to ancient Hebrew New Year liturgies which celebrated the reunion and marriage of the sun god with the mother goddess; (d) *the lyrical,* in which the Song of Songs is considered an anthology of love songs by lovers during courtship, at weddings, and after marriage.

The author thinks that allegorizing is an abuse of scripture (unless the passage being studied is itself an allegory, as the allegories of Ezekiel); the dramatic interpretation makes Solomon a villain chasing a poor peasant girl rather than a hero; the liturgical or cultic seems to distort the songs in the interest of finding their origin in ancient fertility rituals. I suggest that we need to set aside our prudish discomfort as we recognize these songs as expressions of simple delight in the sexuality of mankind. Let the songs speak for themselves, let us not twist or distort them, nor attempt to find mystical and hidden double meanings behind each song.

Part III

GOD'S SAVING ACTION IN HISTORY

In PART I we distinguished between two approaches to history. One perspective seeks to know the social and historical backgrounds of the period being discussed—it seeks to understand the cultural, economic, political, social, religious customs of the day. The second approach includes these concerns, but also looks at the events which take place on this historic stage with the eyes of faith. The man of faith thus sees things which a man lacking faith cannot see. This does not mean that a man of faith reads into the events that which was really not there. On the contrary, his eyes are opened by faith to include the spiritual as well as the physical world.

When the people of Israel "remembered" the events of the patriarchs (Abraham, Isaac, and Jacob), the experiences of Moses on Mt. Sinai, the exodus from Egypt, and the period of wanderings prior to Sinai and in the Wilderness, their thoughts were not centered on the events themselves. Rather, their thoughts were centered on their God, Yahweh, who out of his powerful love had acted in their behalf in each of these events. Thus it was God who called Abraham and gave him the initial promises which were fulfilled during the succeeding centuries. It was God who called Moses at Sinai and told him of the divine concern for the oppressed in Egypt. It was God who delivered Israel from Egypt at the Sea of Reeds. It was God who gave Moses the Ten Commandments ("words") and made a covenant with his chosen people. It was God who gave Israel the land of Canaan—the land promised to Abraham many centuries before. This way of looking at historical events with the eyes of faith (that is, of seeing God's *action* within the historical events) is often referred to as salvation-history.

There are several methods of studying the Old Testament from a theological perspective. One approach assumes that the task is simply one of classifying, organizing, and systematizing the various concepts (God, spirit, man, sin, salvation, and so forth) as found in the Old Testament. This view, though very popular until recent years, has been found inadequate. Another approach to the theological task is christological. This view assumes that the Old Testament is basically concerned with promises and prophecies concerning the Messiah (Christ). This method studies prophecy and fulfillment. Others study the Old Testament seeking persons and events who prefigure the coming of Jesus. Thus, the life of Joseph (his near-death experiences at the hands of his brothers, by Potiphar, and by the Pharaoh while in prison—yet all the time his life being overshadowed by the guiding hand of God), prefigured the providential care of Jesus Christ. Abraham, Joseph, Moses, David, and others become early "types" for understanding Jesus and his sacrificial life for mankind.

In all of these approaches there is the search for the basic unity of the Bible. Sometimes the discovered "unity" is forced or distorted and becomes unreal. It is very easy to make a neat package in which the "unfolding drama of salvation" becomes the only purpose and concern of Old Testament studies, but too often this single-minded approach to the Scriptures overlooks many significant facts and difficulties. For this reason some people are tempted to allegorize those passages which "don't fit" their scheme. This is very dangerous and is very misleading, if not a falsification of the scripture. A good rule to follow is: *Never allegorize a scriptural passage! Let it speak for itself in its context.*

Where then does the unity of the Bible reside? I suggest that the theology and the literature of the Old Testament find unity in the events of God's *election* of, and covenant with, Israel. The books of the Pentateuch are all based on this concept of God's choice of Israel as a chosen people. God elected (chose) them from among all the other nations, not that God disliked other nations or peoples, but he chose Abraham (and finally Israel) that through them, *all mankind* might be drawn unto himself.

Contemporary scholars are convinced that there are several confessions of faith, such as Deut. 26:5-11; and Josh. 24:1-28, which are very ancient, going back to the time before David. These confessions are based on the conviction of Israel that Yahweh her God had chosen, redeemed, and blessed her people. This conviction of divine election, modern scholars believe, must certainly go back even to the days of the patriarchs. So our study of God's saving acts in history will begin with the patriarch, Abraham.

In this study we observe a most fascinating fact: Each generation had to reinterpret the concept of God's election and covenant in terms meaningful for their day. Each generation sought the relevance of this claim for its time. Let us note briefly the reinterpretations that were made as each age sought to make the ancient claim of being God's chosen people relevant.

First was the election of and covenant with Abraham (who was never personally able to claim the land of Canaan promised to him and his heirs). Then the divine election and covenant underwent a fresh reinterpretation when Moses called his people to enter into a covenant with Yahweh at Mt. Sinai. At Sinai the chosen (elected) people assumed moral obligations as an expression of gratitude for the covenant.

When Joshua created the league of twelve tribes at

Shechem, uniting the tribes under the leadership of Yahweh, he interpreted God's election and covenant in ways that were relevant for a new social setting, for most of the Hebrews were now farmers settled on the land, no longer nomads following their flocks.

The election of, and covenant with, David also underwent a fresh reinterpretation. The prophet Nathan reinterpreted the old concepts of a chosen people. He taught that God now chose not so much a people as a dynasty which was intrusted to fulfill justice and maintain the sacred law among the people. Likewise, Deuteronomy and the Deuteronomic writers of the history of Israel, the prophets, and later the author of I and II Chronicles all "updated" their understanding of "election." By "updating" I mean that they were compelled to show how this conviction of their fathers concerning election was relevant for their day— whether in times of prosperity, warfare, exile, or in the difficult days following the return from exile.

And the experiences of reinterpretation of election and covenant did not cease when the Old Testament had been completed. Note how Stephen, for example, based his defense (Acts 7) on God's saving acts in the history of Israel. He described how God had worked out his promise of a "chosen people" through Abraham, Joseph, Moses, David, Solomon, and finally through Jesus. Stephen reinterpreted Israel's conviction of God's election in order to show the relevance of this claim for his (New Testament) days. He sought to deal with Israel's testimony of Yahweh's activity in her historical life.

This is basically a theological problem. Only those with eyes of faith can deal with it adequately, for eyes of faith see more than the simple objective phenomena of events. They see the whole of history as the movement of God and man's response.

Our concern in the chapters which follow is a similar concern: We seek to deal theologically with Israel's claim through the centuries that God had chosen her. As we study the various periods, we shall see how this claim was reinterpreted by the spiritual leaders of each period. In a sense we listen to their testimony concerning Yahweh's relationship to them. The various interpretations, seeking relevance for each succeeding age, suggest the impossibility of a single theological system for the Old Testament. There are many and diverse views. For example, the concept of the chosen people moves from that of the people of Israel, to the chosen seed of David (in the Davidic covenant), to the exiles in Babylon who are the "good figs" in whom the promises reside, to the suffering servant who lays down his life that others might find God. Even so, the conviction of "election" runs as the golden thread through the centuries of faith.

CHAPTER 1

The Election of and Covenant With the Patriarchs

THE IDEA OF THE covenant begins with the patriarchs themselves. Abraham is the source from which the conception of election comes. One of the reasons for believing this is so derives from the study of Josh. 24.

Josh. 24 is considered a brief summary of Israel's concept of salvation inasmuch as it shows God's saving acts in the *history* of Israel: God's call to and leading of the patriarchs, his revelation to Moses and his deliverance of the Hebrews from Egypt, his covenant with them at Sinai, and his guidance in the wilderness at Kadesh-barnea, and finally his giving the Hebrews the land of Canaan. Josh. 24 is considered to be an ancient ritual, used at the cultic center at Shechem (the city in the valley between Mt. Ebal and Mt. Gerizim). It describes what may well have been a renewal ceremony of the covenant—possibly an annual or, more likely, a seven-year (sabbatical) festival, at which time the ritual would be read, and the "words" of Moses repeated and affirmed by Israel.

If these conclusions are correct, then we see in this ancient rite a firm conviction that Abraham was the source of the faith in Israel's election. Josh. 24:2-4 reads:

> And Joshua said to all the people, "Thus says the Lord, the God of Israel, 'Your fathers lived of old beyond the Euphrates, Terah, the father of Abraham and of Nahor; and they served other gods. Then I took your father Abraham from beyond the River

153

and led him through all the land of Canaan, and
made his offspring many. I gave him Isaac; and to
Isaac I gave Jacob and Esau.' "

Here we have an ancient ritual that affirms the covenant
with Abraham.

What was this covenant with Abraham? One of our oldest sources is found in Gen. 12 (J-document), and also
Gen. 15 (both J and E). Fundamentally the covenant is
this: God elected (chose) Abram (later called Abraham),
and told him to go to a new land. If Abraham obeyed, God
would fulfill a threefold promise: (a) God would make
him a great nation—his descendants would be as many as
the sands of the sea; (b) God would give him the land of
Canaan, "the promised land"; and (c) because of Abraham's fidelity, God would bless all mankind through Abraham's descendants. The first six books of the Old Testament deal with this threefold promise and show how all
three provisions were fulfilled by the time of David. Beginning with David, the saving history of Israel was a thing
of the past. The reinterpretation of the claims of the covenant, the meaning of election for that day, now required a
prophet, such as Nathan.

God called Abraham to leave Haran and journey by faith
(see Heb. 11:8) to a new land which God would show him.
This he did, going to the land of Canaan.

On his way to Canaan, Abraham stopped first at Shechem,
a powerful Canaanite city-fortress, which God assured him
would be his in the future. Here he built an altar and
worshiped. (It was at this same place that Joshua, many
centuries later, formed the twelve-tribe league of Israel.
Joshua united under the leadership of Yahweh those tribes
of Jacob who already lived in Canaan with the Joseph
tribes who had just come out of Egypt.) Abraham's construction of altars reminds us of his piety and habit of
worship.

The accounts of Abraham portray him as a man struggling between faith and doubt. At times he is convinced that God will fulfill his promises, yet he shows by his actions that he often doubts God's promise. For example, after being assured that the land will be his, Abraham forsakes it during a famine and goes to Egypt (Gen. 12:10-20), or Gerar (Gen. 20). He gets into trouble in each case and is saved by divine intervention of Yahweh. Abraham proves to be unworthy upon several occasions: For instance, he questions whether he will ever have an heir (since he and his wife are too old for children), and he treats Hagar, mother of his son Ishmael, in an unworthy manner.

But in spite of it all, if not *because of* his struggles of faith, Abraham comes through as a man of firm conviction. He is convinced of the guiding hand of God throughout his journeys and is assured that God's promises will be fulfilled in the days of his posterity. Abraham's confidence in God is stated by the very name of God, whom he calls "The Shield of Abraham" (Gen. 15:1). In the various instances in his life where fear would be natural—as in warfare, or before the pharaoh, or in concern for his aging son (who, still unmarried, was to bear sons of promise)—in each case God was to be his "shield" so he was not to fear. He was to trust God whose providence would meet all dire circumstances in life.

Perhaps the greatest testing of his life was the occasion when he felt God calling him to sacrifice his only son, Isaac, on the altar. His willingness to give God the very best that he had—even when the victim was to be his only son—and, even more significantly, the child in whom God's promise would be fulfilled—proved his willingness to be obedient under all conditions. Once again, the promises were reaffirmed (Gen. 22:1-19).

A word should be said about the covenant. The characteristic feature about the patriarchal covenant was the relationship between God and the patriarch. All God asked of the patriarch was his trust. The covenant made no demands concerning the *place* where the covenant was made.

God could be worshiped not only at Shechem but also at Bethel or Beersheba or Hebron—at any place and at any time! In fact, as the J-tradition suggests, Abraham seems to have preferred prayer to sacrifices. In God's election (choosing) of and covenant with Abraham and his descendants, God pledged himself to care for them, lead them, give them a good land and a great posterity. It is interesting to note that, apparently, no moral demands were made on the part of Abraham. Abraham was simply offered a "gift" of grace by God. Even when he struggled with doubts, God's offer of providence and assurance of election were not removed. A covenant was generally concluded by an expression of *shalom,* often translated "peace," which probably meant that a sense of rightness and reconciliation had been established.

The faith of the fathers was predicated solely on God's action in their behalf and not on their loyalty. It was to be different with Moses, who received the ten "words." [1] Once the covenant was accepted, a response on the part of the people toward the ten words was expected.

The patriarchs—Abraham, Isaac, and Jacob—worshiped God, though they called him by different titles. Abraham called him the "Shield of Abraham" (Gen. 15:1); Isaac called him the "Fear of Isaac" (Gen. 31:42); while Jacob called him the "Mighty One" or El Shaddai (Gen. 49:24). It was Moses who pointed out that these three names did not represent three different Gods, but all referred to one God, whom he called Yahweh.

Without doubt, Joseph carried the patriarchal promises with him to Egypt, where they were treasured through the centuries. The Joseph stories portray him as greatly impressed by God's guiding hand—so much so that he readily forgave his brothers because of God's hidden, but just and assuring, actions in his life.

---

[1] The Old Testament does not refer to the Ten Commandments as such. Rather, they are called the ten "words." The later expansion of these ten "words" are referred to as statutes and commandments.

Apparently the members of the clan of Levi (from southern Judah), who had been defeated in warfare and almost destroyed as a tribe, joined the Joseph tribes at Goshen in Egypt shortly before the time of Moses. Moses' parents were from this tribe of Levi. They, too, with the Joseph tribes, would have treasured the revelation of God's election of Abraham and his descendants. We are ready now to see how this faith-claim of election was made relevant for faith in Moses' time.

CHAPTER 2

God's Saving Action in Redeeming His Chosen People From Egypt

In Part I we saw how the Joseph tribe, elevated to power during the reign of the Hyksos, was put to slave labor under Seti I, the Egyptian Pharaoh "who knew not Joseph." We also noted that Moses, the adopted "prince of Egypt," had killed an Egyptian and fled to Midian for safety. Here he married the daughter of Jethro, a priest in Midian, and settled down to the life of a shepherd and possibly that of a coppersmith (since "Kenite," the group he joined in Midian, means "smith").

Beginning with a very great religious experience, Moses became the real founder of the Hebrew religion. Through Moses God was able to lead his Chosen People from slavery to the promised land—to the land of Canaan, promised to the patriarchs. In this divine activity in Israel's history, several important and distinct events occurred with which we shall deal separately: Moses' religious experience at Mt. Sinai; the deliverance of Israel at the Sea of Reeds; the revelations of Yahweh at Mt. Sinai; and Yahweh's guidance in the wilderness.

Moses' Religious Experience

While a shepherd for Jethro, Moses guided his sheep for pasture near Mt. Sinai. There he became aware of the presence of God, and, in Oriental style, took off his shoes (as we might take off our hats) in recognition of the divine presence.

Moses' background was a most interesting one. Born of a Hebrew family (his father was a Levite), and undoubtedly trained in the faith of the patriarchs, he knew well the threefold promise made to Abraham. He knew also that his people, now enslaved, yearned to return to Canaan and fulfill the promises once made to them, the descendants of Abraham. Our biblical traditions state that Moses was reared as a prince of Egypt. As such he would have been trained to fulfill the role of a foreman of great estates, learning the scribal skills of writing and elementary mathematics, law, and military strategy. He, of course, would have known of the religions of Egypt—and of the striving for monotheism of the great reformer, Akh-en-Aton, who lived a generation before him. What the future might have held for Moses had he not killed an Egyptian is hard to say, but it is hardly possible that he would have achieved in Egypt as much as he did as the leader of a group of slaves who yearned to return to their homeland.

Moses had a creative mind; he was more than just a shepherd of sheep and goats. His mind was active, concerned with memories of both the luxury of Egypt's royalty and the lowly conditions of its suffering slaves. It is most enlightening to note that in Moses' religious experience on Mt. Sinai, the first revelation that came to him was that the God of the fathers was one Being! How often this religious genius must have pondered the validity of Akh-en-Aton's monotheistic reform! How often, too, Moses must have pondered about the three names which the patriarchs used as they prayed: the Shield of Abraham, the Fear of Isaac, and the Mighty One of Jacob. Were they three gods, or three manifestations of one God? In this great moment at Sinai, Moses learned that "I am the God of your father, the God of Abraham, the God of Isaac, and the God of Jacob" (Exod. 3:6). God is One!

Second, Moses learned that the God of the fathers, before whom he was now bowing, was concerned about the oppressed. God had heard the cry of his people, he knew of their sufferings, and he desired to deliver them. God is a redeeming God. God also intended to fulfill his three-fold promises made to Abraham through these slaves in Egypt, and wanted to give the Hebrews their "promised land" of Canaan.

Third, Moses learned that the name of "the God of the fathers" was Yahweh. It was the first time that this name was identified with the names used by Abraham, Isaac, and Jacob. Apparently the name Yahweh had been used previously, even occasionally in Palestine, and quite prob-ably by Jethro of Midian. The revelation of the name of God—Yahweh—was very significant for Moses. To know the name of the deity was to have assurance of his presence when he needed him.

How we wish we knew the exact meaning of the word "Yahweh." Some scholars interpret the name Yahweh in philosophical terms, having to do with *Essence* and *Being*. But the Hebrews were not philosophically minded. Others suggest that Yahweh meant not what he *was* in his inner nature, but what he would show himself to be to Israel. He would declare himself through his actions. Some have sug-gested that Exod. 3:14 should simply read: "I am Yahweh!" (rather than "I am who I am," or "I will be what I will be").

This latter suggestion arises out of the fact that by about 250 B.C. Jews had begun to avoid pronouncing the divine name. Others have suggested that the divine name, Yahweh, simply means "I will be there (with you), whenever needed." We do not know which interpretation is correct. The author leans toward the latter two views, but prefers simply "I am Yahweh." (Note that Moses said to Pharaoh, "Thus says *Yahweh,* the God of Israel, let my people go.") The rest of ch. 3 of the book of Exodus delineates God's nature as one who will "be there" when needed, and also as one who is known by his actions.

Perhaps we can anticipate the Ten Commandments a bit by noting that the name of Yahweh was of exceedingly great importance to Moses in another way. Whereas Egypt had many gods—such as the cat, cow, crocodile, and falcon—and therefore also many images, Moses was told not to make any images of Yahweh whatsoever. When men prayed, they were to call upon "the name of Yahweh," rather than to call to some image! So the *name* replaces the image in Mosaic religion. To call upon his name is to be assured that he is there. What a unique contribution to religion!

This imageless religion was observed in the days of Abraham, who lived in a time when men worshiped many gods and built images of each. Gen. 12:8 tells how Abraham moved from Shechem to Bethel, where he pitched his tent, erected an altar, and without images, called on "the name of the Lord." (Note also Gen. 13:4; 21:33.) For this reason Israel never had an image of God in the Holy of Holies. Rather, the people conceived of the invisible but ever-present Yahweh as residing between the cherubs which guarded the Ark of the Covenant. Christians greatly value this concept when we pray "Hallowed be thy name" (that is, hallowed be thy presence).

Deliverance at the Sea of Reeds

Yahweh commanded Moses and Aaron, who had apparently escaped from slavery in Egypt, to return to Egypt and to present his demands to Pharaoh (Ramses II). After many presentations of Yahweh's demands, the slaves were permitted to leave under the leadership of Moses.

Having left Rameses, the capital of Egypt, and the city which these slaves had helped to build, Moses led his motley group southward to Succoth, another military depot, then east for a few miles, then back northward again to the waters of Lake Menzaleh.[1]

The crossing of the Sea of Reeds was the greatest event in the life of Israel—for it assured them that Yahweh

---

[1] See page 28 for further explication of the exodus from Goshen.

would actually care for and protect them. This event gave
the Hebrews the guarantee that God was with them (he
had said: "I will be with you") and it also assured them
that he would be so in the future.

We ought to be aware that there are several interpretations in Exod. 14 as to "how" the event took place. These
varieties are due to the fact each of the three sources in
Exodus (J, E, and P) has a theological point of view as to
how the even took place. All three agree, of course, on the
fact of the crossing! One suggests that "a strong east wind"
blew the waters back so that the former slaves could walk
across the bottom of the lake dry-shod. But it was more than
a strong east wind, it was *Yahweh* who had directed that
wind. *He* had brought their salvation. Hence, the oldest
confessional creeds (Deut. 26:5-8 and Josh. 24:6-7) make
much of Yahweh's having taken part in their first warfare
—in fact, they would have been destroyed had he not in-
tervened. In a sense this event was the birthnight of the
nation. Back of the physical event Moses and his people
saw the saving activity of God in their historical life.

Yahweh's Revelations at Mt. Sinai

After his first experience with Yahweh on Mt. Sinai,
Moses returned to Egypt, appealing first to the slaves to respond to Yahweh's call to return to Canaan to receive the
land promised to the patriarchs. Then he appealed to
Ramses II, till finally he granted the slaves their freedom.
After the crossing of the Reed Sea, Moses led these former
slaves, possibly six thousand persons, to Mt. Sinai. Here
again he sought an experience with Yahweh—this time not
for himself but for guidance for the large group of people
he was leading toward Canaan. His people were fully aware
that they were the chosen people—the descendants of
Abraham. They had experienced Yahweh's saving action
at the Sea of Reeds. They were uncertain, however, about
the future.

Theologically, the important event at Mt. Sinai was the revelation to the people. But the content of this revelation differs according to the source (JE, P, or D) being studied. This means that we find several different kinds of revelations given at Sinai, recorded in Exod. 19:1–Num. 10:10. First, there are laws regulating the more-or-less everyday problems of life, as found in the Book of the Covenant (Exod. 20:22–23:19 and in Deuteronomy). There are also ordinances which deal almost solely with the cult—priestly material as found in both Exodus and Numbers, especially with the prescriptions for the Tabernacle, priestly apparel, and manner of offerings and their regulation.

The priestly material emphasizes the fact that Yahweh dwells ("tabernacles") with Israel and may be found in the tent of meeting. Just as God led, protected, and cared for the patriarchs, so he will provide and care for his chosen people now. What God did in the past, he now assumes again in the present. All the intricate paraphernalia for the Tabernacle and its services are geared to emphasize the fact that the glory of God is with them and will continue to be with them.

The cultic regulations, the secular statutes of the Book of the Covenant, and the ten "words" form the basic regulations for their life with Yahweh.[2] For our purposes the Ten Commandments are the most significant.

The first four commandments deal with man's relationship to God, while the last six deal with man's relationship with his fellowman. We must frankly admit that the last six were not really new in the legal and ethical systems of mankind. These had appeared in other law books and moral codes prior to this period—in Babylonia, Sumer, and Egypt. The first four of the Ten Commandments, however, are truly unique, as we shall note a little later.

First, let us note the context in which the Ten Commandments seem to have been given and used in later

---

[2] See page 156, footnote 1.

generations. In later years, in the time of the judges, there apparently was a pilgrimage festival at Shechem every seven years (Deut. 31:10-11), at which time Israel renewed her covenant with Yahweh (see Deut. 26:5-9, Josh. 24:2-8). The reciting of the decalogue seems to have been a very important part of such a festival. We are impressed by how contemporary the reading of the Law is made for *each* generation:

> "The Lord our God made a covenant with us in Horeb. *Not* with *our fathers* did the Lord make this covenant, but with *us,* who are all of us here alive this day. The Lord spoke with *you* face to face at the mountain, out of the midst of the fire." (Deut. 5:24, italics added).

The renewal of the covenants was considered to be more than acceptance of a burdensome set of laws. Thus, Deut. 30:15 suggests that the renewal of the covenant was a time for decision making by Israel—a decision for life or for death. This meant that the Ten Commandments were considered a gift from God—a gift of life! It was the total community—priests and laity, not the priests alone—who made these pilgrimages; the priests and laity made a decision every seven years for life or death. In choosing life and thus affirming the Ten Commandments, Israel also affirmed the saving events by which God first gave the ten "words" to Moses.

Reading backward, then, from the pilgrimage festivals to the original giving of the Ten Commandments at Sinai, we need to view the context as one of the saving acts of God. God was giving his chosen people a way that would lead to life. We observe that most of the commandments are negative. Israel was not to do those things which displeased God. What Israel ought to do is left open for further thinking. But, if Israel would please Yahweh, then there are some things she would not do—commit adultery, steal, make false oaths, and so forth. In not displeasing God, she is also choosing life for herself. Each generation, in renewing the covenant at Shechem, affirmed the "way of life" for their lives. They did not let their fathers choose for them; they had to choose for themselves. This was certainly the wisest of pedagogy!

If the above descriptions of the pilgrimage festivals are correct, then it would seem to follow that the Israelites did not regard the Ten Commandments as a burdensome ethical code, but as a gift of life from God. For this gift the people lifted up songs of praise and thanksgiving.

The generations following the period of Moses affirmed the Ten Commandments for their lives. Yet, each generation not only felt obligated to participate in the renewal festival itself, but also felt free to reinterpret the meaning of the covenant and the fact of God's election of them as the chosen people for their day.

Now, let us look at the first four of the Ten Commandments, for they are truly unique in the history of religion. The first commandment, "You shall have no other gods before me" (Deut. 5:7), must be viewed in the light of Yahweh's election of Israel and his actions in history in her behalf. For Israel, God had proven himself to be the only God by way of his saving acts to the patriarchs, to the Joseph tribes at the exodus, the Reed Sea, and at Sinai.

We wonder if Akh-en-Aton's belief in one God influenced Moses. Moses was trained in the religious thought of the Egyptians, as well as other disciplines. It may well be that his firm faith in Yahweh made him categorically deny Akh-en-Aton's claim that Aton was the only God. This denial against Akh-en-Aton's claim could well have been the seed for Israel's monotheism. Nonetheless, Moses' faith grew out of the divine events in Israel's behalf, not out of intellectual arguments.

This demand for intolerance of other gods was unique in Moses' day, though Akh-en-Aton had had a similar idea a generation before him. The general attitude in Moses' day was that the various gods could be worshiped without incurring jealousy on the part of any one god. Not so with Yahweh, whose emotions were like those of a lover. He wanted and required single-minded loyalty and devotion. (Psychologically, we see the validity of this point.) We must remember that this concept of intolerance was not "dreamed up" by Moses, but is a faith-claim of revelation concerning Yahweh's will toward his chosen people.

The second commandment likewise is unique: "You shall not make for yourself a graven image, or any likeness of anything that is in heaven above, or that is on the earth beneath" (Deut. 5:8). The uniqueness of this commandment lies in the fact that Israel believed in an invisible God. Human eye cannot see him, nor can the hand touch him, nor is he located (and thus limited) in some place in space.

When Moses returned to Israel from Mt. Sinai with the tablets of the ten words, he discovered that Aaron had molded a golden calf from the earrings, necklaces, anklets, and other jewelry of the people. Moses was furious. Aaron had formed an image of Yahweh, modeling his likeness to one of the gods of Egypt—possibly Apis the bull, or Hathor, the cow-headed goddess of fertility and love. Yahweh, however, was not to be likened to any physical thing—whether the sun disk, or the bull, or the crocodile. God was pronounced to be invisible.[3] So it was that Moses, in righteous anger, feeling that Yahweh had been affronted by such an image, broke the tablets of the Law on the rocks below him.

No physical form of God had been displayed when Yahweh acted in Israel's behalf against Pharaoh; nor when Yahweh acted to deliver the Joseph tribes from the Sea of Reeds; nor when he called them before himself at Mt. Sinai. Yahweh's spirit was invisible, and in no way could

---

[3] Exod. 33:23 illustrates a seemingly illogical statement of the concept of the invisible God. But before we allow ourselves to be too critical, recall that the Apostles' Creed states that Jesus is seated at the *right hand* of God. We too often use anthropomorphisms to express the ineffable. The point here is that God is different from his creations, which are physical.

God be portrayed in a physical image. Yahweh revealed his nature only through his acts. Yahweh, therefore, was not to be known by way of an image, but *by his saving acts in history*. All the early creeds emphasize this aspect of God's self-revelation to Israel. It is precisely because history is the basic means of God's revelation that the concept of worshiping Yahweh through images is impossible! The proper way of worshiping God was to acknowledge his saving acts in the past, and to sing praises of gratitude for his loving kindness as expressed through those actions.

Previously we have noted that neither the Tabernacle nor Solomon's Temple housed an image. Instead of calling on the name of some image (Baal, Hathor, Horus, Astarte, or Apis) the Israelites called on "the name of the Lord (Yahweh)." In so doing they became aware of his awesome presence, for he had promised, "I will be with you."

Israel's refusal to make an image and her affirmation of history as Yahweh's mode of revelation had great effects on her theology. God was conceived to be a transcendent deity. This meant that his self-revelation was different from that of other gods. Thus Deut. 4:9-20 declares that Yahweh revealed his will through his "words" which he spoke at Sinai. This conception of God's revelation via the spoken word eventually became the basis for "the Word of the Lord" of the prophets, the late Deuteronomists, and Second Isaiah.

Concerning the third commandment, "You shall not take the name of the Lord your God in vain" (Deut. 5-11), we recall the importance given to "the name." Instead of images, Israel called on the *name* of the Lord—and thus was assured of his presence. This third commandment refers fundamentally to the taking of oaths, at which time a man might call on the name (that is, the presence of) the Lord as witness to his sincerity and intent. A person who called on God ("the name of the Lord") as a witness was obligated to fulfill his vow or oath. He should not take the name of the Lord—God's presence as a witness—

lightly! We of our day have stretched the original meaning of this commandment considerably when we make it refer to the use of the divine name in a curse. The intent of this third commandment is to indicate the solemnity with which one should take his vows.

The fourth commandment, as with the preceding three commandments, deals with man's relationship to God. It is concerned with hallowing the Sabbath. The creation of the world may be considered the first of God's "mighty acts" in behalf of mankind. Men are to hallow the seventh day of the week as an expression of gratitude for God's creative work in preparing for their lives.

The command concerning the observance of the Sabbath has both religious and secular motivations. The observance is motivated for religious purposes—honoring God and hallowing his Sabbath—and also for secular purposes: Mankind needs regular periods of rest from the steady grind of work. Without such Sabbath rest, mankind faces unrelieved tensions which find release in bitterness, jealousy, hatred, and spiritual rebellion.

The remaining six commandments deal with man's relationship to man. In contrast to the first four commandments, which were unique with Israel, the last six commandments are found in other codes of ethics and laws, such as the Code of Hammurabi and the Egyptian *Book of the Dead*. This fact, however, does not minimize the importance of these six commandments. Except for the fifth commandment ("Honor your father and your mother. . . .") they are all negative—"thou shalt not. . . ." They are apparently in this form because they state that which is displeasing to God, namely: murder, adultery, stealing, false witness, covetousness.

As stated previously, these negative commandments are to help Israel maintain right relationships with God. We must observe that they do not give the affirmative demands which Yahweh requires of man. Perhaps this is part of the uniqueness of Israel's relationship with God, inasmuch as what God does require is left to man's searching. The last five commandments clearly state what God *does not* want man to do if he is to have life, but it leaves open what God *does* want man to do. Even so, the commandments are set in the context of the covenant which God has made with man. What man does to or with, or through, other men must be in harmony with this context.

All Ten Commandments should be viewed against the background of Israel's experience at Sinai—these commandments were a gift from Yahweh to Israel in order that she might have life (as contrasted with death which is the alternative if she lived contrary to these "words"). From this point of view then, the Ten Commandments are a part of the saving acts of God in the historical life of Israel.

Israel's acceptance of these ten "words" at Sinai should not be viewed legalistically, for the unity of the people was religious, not political. The format—the structure—of the Ten Commandments was based upon the accepted legal structures of suzerain treaties of the fourteenth and thirteenth centuries, which Moses would have known very well from his studies in legal matters in Egypt, when he was a student.[4]

Yahweh's Guidance in the Wilderness

The gift of the Ten Commandments was but the beginning of God's revelation of his will to his chosen people. The early traditions (Exod. 33 and 34)[5] tell how God revealed himself to Moses and through him to his people by way of the tent of meeting.

The tent of meeting was the place where Moses was to go to "meet" with Yahweh. It was the place of encounter

---

[4] See Part I, page 32 for the form of suzerain treaties. Note the great similarities in style between these treaties and the Ten Commandments.

[5] The reader might profit from marking his Bible according to the sources beginning with the Ten Commandments:

E-tradition Exod. 20:1–23:33; 24:3-8, 12-15, 18b, 32:1-35; 33:3b-11

J-tradition Exod. 24:1-2, 9-11; 33:1-3a, 12-34:28

P-tradition Exod. 24:15b-18b; 25:1–31:18; 34:29-40:30

(Exod. 33:7), primarily a place for obtaining divine oracles or judgments and directions from Yahweh. Once they were received, Moses proclaimed the "Word" of Yahweh to the people. Theologically you could say the tent of meeting was the place where God manifested himself, making his will known.

The tent of meeting (Exod. 33:7-11, E) is quite different from the Tabernacle (Exod. 35–40, P). Recall that the Priestly tradition, set down in the fifth century B.C. (using old traditions, to be sure), was a reinterpretation of God's act of choosing and covenanting with Israel. The "author" of this tradition wrote to show the relevance of these savings acts which God performed during Moses' time for his own day, eight hundred years after the event. For that reason the priests' description of the Tabernacle is quite different from the description of the tent of meeting of the early tradition.

In the E-tradition the tent of meeting was pitched outside the camp whereas the Priestly Code always considered it at the center of the camp. The tent of meeting was not considered the place where Yahweh dwelt with his people as was the case with the Tabernacle and later with Solomon's Temple. It was the place where Moses went to meet with God—to know his will, his purposes and to receive his Word that Moses might proclaim it to the people.

The Ark was the cultic object which represented the place where the presence was located. The Ark was approximately fifty inches long, thirty inches wide, and thirty inches deep. It was a rectangular wooden box, probably overlaid with gold. Rings were attached high up on the side of the Ark, so that long poles could be thrust through them, permitting priests to carry the Ark. (A similar beautifully carved and painted box is found in the Cairo Museum from the days of King Tutankhamen. The god Anubis is seated on top of the box. It also was carried by two long poles through rings in the sides of the box.)

The Ark of the Covenant was a distinctive box, for it

symbolized the presence of Yahweh with his people. A cherub was carved on each side of the Ark. A picture of the throne of a Canaanite king in this same period found at Megiddo shows the throne with two cherubs, one on either side of the throne, forming the arms of the throne. (A cherub is a composite creature: It has the head of a man, wings of an eagle, body of a lion, and legs and hooves of an ox.) The king was seated in between the cherubs.

In similar fashion, the Ark, with two cherubs placed on each side, was considered the throne of the invisible Yahweh. It was the place where God's presence was recognized as being ("the ark of the covenant of the Lord of hosts, who is enthroned on the cherubim," I Sam. 4:4). When a person wanted to consult God, even in the days of David, and especially in the days of Solomon following the time of David, he went to the Ark. The Ark was consulted by priests before moving the camp in the wilderness experiences, and it was carried into the center of battle during warfare. In short, it was the most sacred cultic object, since it symbolized the presence of God.

We ought to note that there were many arks, but only one "Ark of the Covenant." The Ark was made even more precious by being the receptacle for Moses' Ten Commandments. It may be that "samples" of manna and Aaron's rod were also put in it. The other arks, as differentiated from the Ark of the Covenant, were used by priests in answering questions by means of the sacred lots, Urim and Thummim (for example, I Sam. 14:16-42). Generally, each priest had his own ark. Since the Ark of the Covenant symbolized the presence of God, one can imagine the joy with which David brought the Ark to Jerusalem, his new capital and religious center (II Sam. 6:12-15). About four hundred years later the Priestly Code stated that the Ark of the Covenant was housed in the tent of meeting (Num. 7:89). Originally they were separated and had different functions. Later they were unified in function.

The Ten Commandments, the tent of meeting, and the

Ark were all considered as given by God to his chosen people in order that they might know him and his will for their lives. In each, God was seen as active in the historical life of his people. We should keep in mind the fact that the community formed at Sinai and in the wilderness was a religious community, not a political one—even though the form of the covenant (see "suzerainty" treaty of Part I) and the form of community organization were borrowed from the cultures of that day.

CHAPTER 3

Reinterpretations in the Days
of the Conquest

HAVING SPENT APPROXIMATELY a year (Exod. 19:1 and Num. 10:11) at Sinai, the people finally started their trek toward Canaan, the land of Promise. Moving toward the northern tip of the Gulf of Aqabah (the eastern finger of the Red Sea), they went directly northward, then veered to the west till they came to a region known as Kadesh-barnea.

At Kadesh-barnea, spies were sent to Canaan. Their purpose was to report back to Moses on the best military tactics for conquering the land (Num. 13-14; Deut. 1:19-21). But a rebellion broke out because the Israelites were afraid of those who lived in Canaan. Archaeological research in our own time has shown that these cities were large and well constructed, often with walls fifty feet high protectively surrounding them, and well defended. "We seemed to ourselves like grasshoppers, and so we seemed to them" (Num. 13:33) was the spies report! This sense of insignificance showed a lack of trust in Yahweh's power. The people had overlooked Moses' confident faith that Yahweh would be with them in warfare even as he had been at the Sea of Reeds. The result: They must stay in the wilderness one year for each day the spies had been in Canaan—forty years! A new generation would enter Canaan, replacing the faithless followers of Moses.

The Wilderness Experience

Later, religious leaders in Israel were to say that God was with his people in their trials in the wilderness, though the Hebrews did not seem to know it at the time (see Num. 14). Centuries later Amos voiced the faith: "I led you forty years in the wilderness" (Amos 2:10; Ps. 136:16). During these forty years the people were to learn what ten of the spies had overlooked: Their successes were not to be the fruit of their own power but of the power of God.' The theological emphasis of this period in the wilderness was the action of God, and the passivity of the people.' The people are notably silent and passive in the decisions made for them during these years in the wilderness.

The prophets of later centuries interpreted this period in the wilderness from two points of view. Hosea and Jeremiah both thought of this period as a time when Israel's relationship with God was at its very best—it was the time of the first love between Yahweh and his beloved Israel (Hos. 11:1, 3; Jer. 2:1-3). Israel had not yet been tempted by other gods, she had trusted completely in Yahweh for her needs—both physical and spiritual. The other view however sees this forty years in the wilderness as a time of judgment and punishment. Deut. 8:15-18 and Jeremiah refer to the terrible life Israel lived in this place of "pits . . . of drought and . . . darkness . . . that none passes through, where no man dwells" (Jer. 2:6). Ezek. 20 and some of the Psalms, for example, Ps. 106, point to the dark hours of Israel's doubt in these days—her murmuring, discontent, faithlessness and finally her judgment. So Ezekiel reinterpreted these wilderness experiences in terms of judgment—and used them as a text for preaching that the people of his time would face a similar wilderness experience if they continued in faithlessness to God (Ezek. 20:35-36). As a matter of fact, his prophecy was upheld too— for Judah was taken into captivity in 597 and 587 B.C. by Nebuchadnezzar of Babylon.

The common theme of the Hexateuch (the first six books of the Old Testament, Genesis through Joshua) is the claim that Yahweh was with Israel, loved her, and would redeem her, giving her people their promised land after their wilderness experience.

At the close of this wilderness experience, Moses led his people to the River Zered (at the southeastern tip of the Dead Sea), and up its valley (thus not traversing the land of Edom) till they came to the eastern boundaries of Edom and Moab. Here they turned northward, conquered the Amorite kingdom, and prepared to enter the "land of promise." Moses died on Mt. Nebo shortly after anointing Hoshea (whom he renamed Joshua—"Yahweh will save") as his successor. [1]

Formation of the Twelve-tribe League (amphictyony)

The chosen people, looking at the land of promise from the heights of Mt. Nebo, were prepared for this last major act of the saving acts of God in the fulfillment of his promises made to Abraham. As promised to Abraham (Gen. 12, 15, 17), his seed had multiplied till they had become a vast number of people, a nation. God had blessed Israel through the giving of his revelations at Sinai and now he was giving them the land of Cannan.

In Part I we noted the threefold thrust of Joshua's military plan to capture the land.[2] Our concern in this section is with the theology of this undertaking, conceived as one of God's acts in the historical life of Israel.[3]

Again we turn to the ancient creeds of Deut. 26:5-9 and Josh. 24. The final act mentioned in these confessional creeds is concerned with God's fulfillment of his promise to Abraham concerning the land:

> And you shall make response before the Lord your God, "A wandering Aramean was my father; and he went down into Egypt and sojourned there, few

in number; and there he became a nation, great,
mighty, and populous. And the Egyptians treated us
harshly, and afflicted us, and laid upon us hard
bondage. Then we cried to the Lord [that is, Yahweh]
the God of our fathers, and the Lord heard our voice,
and saw our affliction, our toil, and our oppression;
and the Lord brought us out of Egypt with a mighty
hand and an outstretched arm, with great terror, with
signs and wonders; and he brought us into this place
and gave us this land, a land flowing with milk and
honey" (Deut. 26:5-9).

This confessional creed is a very ancient one. It was apparently recited at the annual (or sabbatical) festival at
Shechem and possibly at Gilgal. Therefore, the thought that
Yahweh "gave" the land of Canaan to his people is quite
old. It is quite obvious that the land had previously belonged to the Canaanites. This concept that God could
give the land belonging to another nation to his chosen
people presupposes a concept not referred to heretofore:
Yahweh is in control of history. Though thinkers of a later
century were to work out the concept of Yahweh as the
Lord of history, the seed of this concept is here, for Yahweh
redistributed the land—taking it from the Canaanites,
Amorites, Ammonites, and others, giving it to Israel.

Yahweh—not the people—is considered the real owner
of the land. This concept was to be enunciated in greater
detail in the times of the monarchy when the question
arose as to whether Baal owned the land. The prophets
Elijah, Hosea, and others proclaimed that only Yahweh
owned the land, and he alone determined fertility. Being
the owner of the land, Yahweh had every right to assign
the land to the various tribes of Jacob, even before the land
was conquered. Here we note the theological claim of
faith that even this act of apportionment of land was one
of God's saving acts in the historical life of Israel.

The confessional *credo*, quoted from Deut. 26 [1] was ob-

---

[1] See page 106.

viously a part of a cultic ritual, for it preceded the giving of tithes (Deut. 26:9-11). With Josh. 24 these very ancient *credos* give us insights as to the cultic acts through which the tribes become one people, Israel. When Joshua had victoriously conquered many of the Canaanite strongholds (though certainly not all), he called an assembly at Shechem, the city between Mt. Ebal and Mt. Gerizim, where Abraham had built his first altar in Cannan. To this assembly at Shechem came two sets of tribes.'One group was composed of those who had left Egypt prior to the time of Moses, possibly at the time when the Egyptians drove out the Hyksos rulers, about 1580 B.C.'These tribes had settled in Canaan, for the most part around Shechem, pasturing their sheep and goats in the hill country of Canaan.[1] They were coexisting with the Canaanites who were well protected in their great walled cities.'The second group of tribes which came to this first general assembly at Shechem were the new tribes who had been in slavery in Egypt and had been led out by Moses.'

Joshua called the assembly in order to unite these two related groups into one religious community.'Basically it was a union of the Leah tribes and the Rachel tribes.' Josh. 24:1-24 tells of this great religious festival at Shechem, the formation of the twelve-tribe community of Yahweh—a religious, not a political union. Josh. 8:30-35 tells how Joshua divided the people into two large groups on either side of the Ark, which was in the center of the valley, between Ebal and Gerizim. Half the people were on one side of the Ark toward Ebal, and the other half on the other side of the Ark toward Gerizim. Here they renewed the covenant made at Mt. Sinai.

The Leah tribes were forced to a decision by the Rachel tribes: either accept or reject Yahweh as your God and do

---

[1] Recall that there were some descendants of Abraham who had not gone with Jacob to Egypt. These apparently settled around Shechem where Abraham had built his first altar in the land of Canaan. Some of this group came with those who had returned under the expulsion of the Hyksos to form the confederacy with those Hebrews under Joshua's command.

so now (Josh. 24:23-25). With their acceptance, they agreed
to lay aside all foreign gods and worship Yahweh only.
This, of course, was to create difficulty for the Leah tribes,
who had been taught to worship the Canaanite Baals (who
were conceived to be the lords, or owners, of the land, and
who therefore controlled fertility). During the later centuries the prophets had to interpret their faith in Yahweh
so that the people could see that Yahweh, not Baal, governed not only history but the fertility of the land and
fecundity of their flocks.

Loyalty to Yahweh was promoted by requiring regular
(seven year) renewals of the covenant. These pilgrimages
were significant for purposes of unifying the clans in their
common loyalty to Yahweh. At these harvest festivals the
Israelites dedicated themselves to Yahweh and to his will for
justice. This renewal of the covenant required the identification with the faith of the fathers (Abraham, Isaac, and
Jacob), a statement about Yahweh's saving acts in the past,
a recitation of the decalogue, a challenge of blessings or
cursings according to their loyalty or disloyalty to Yahweh,
and subscription to an oath to be loyal to Yahweh. ʾ

This process of renewal meant that each generation had
to assume the covenant for themselves; it was not to be
passed mechanically from generation to generation. Each
man, each family, each tribe, had to make his own covenant
with God. Note the relevance, the contemporaneity, for
each generation as they said "Not *with our fathers* did the
Lord make this covenant, but with *us,* who are all of us
here alive this day" (Deut. 5:3 italics added).

It is interesting to observe that many scholars think that
the name "Israel" was accepted at this time by this larger
body of Yahweh's chosen people. This name had not been
given at Sinai, but was assumed by the union of the tribes
under Yahweh at Shechem by Joshua.ʾ

During this period the tribes were bound together by
ties of religious loyalty to Yahweh but were held together
as individual tribes by the authority of charismatic leaders

called "judges." These men were called of God to their responsibilities; hence, they were considered more gifted than ordinary men. None of the judges ever ruled all the tribes at one time, nor was there a dynasty established by any one of them.[2] They were known especially for their military prowess and sometimes for their ability to bring reconciliation between persons or groups within a tribe who claimed some injustice had been done them, as, for example, Deborah. Their authority was recognized as having come from God. They were divinely gifted, hence *charismatic*.

The book of Judges recounts many stories of how Yahweh won holy wars by directing his judges. Gideon, Japheth, Deborah and Barak, Ehud, and Shamgar are some of the judges through whom Yahweh's power brought victory to Israel. Israel was convinced that Yahweh, whose saving acts had been so great and powerful in the past, was still at work in their day too. Though the saving acts of Yahweh had fulfilled the promises made to Abraham, God's concern and care continued with his chosen people even after the fulfillment of the promises.

Moses and his people at Sinai and Kadesh-barnea looked forward to the future when Yahweh would fulfill his promises made to Abraham, but each of the judges and his people looked back to the relatively recent past and offered prayers of gratitude for those saving events and prayers for God's continuing presence in their day. The emphasis now was not what God would do in the future, but what God had already done. This meant a reinterpretation of the relationship between Yahweh and his people. The judges and priests had to show the relevance of the Mosaic faith for their day, and this they did in part through the annual and sabbatical religious festivals at various shrines.

There was not just one shrine at this time. Men wor-

---

[2] Gideon's son (Judges 9–10) unsuccessfully attempted it. Samuel (1 Sam. 8:1-9) apparently desired to establish a dynasty through his sons too, but to no avail.

shiped at Hebron, Shechem, Gilgal, Bethel, Shiloh, and many other places. However, the focal point was always the shrine at which the Ark of the Covenant rested. It was now apparently housed in the tent of meeting. Sacrifices were made before the tent, and the people came there to receive oracles from the holy Ark through the priests, where Yahweh's presence could be found. The tent of meeting which housed the Ark was pitched at different places during the period of the judges. It was at Gilgal shortly after crossing the Jordan River, then at Bethel (Judg. 20:18, 26-27), and then at Shiloh (I Sam. 1-4), where we find the young boy Samuel ministering to the needs of Eli the priest. Finally, after the destruction of Shiloh, the Philistines, who had invaded Canaan in 1192 B.C. and captured the holy Ark, returned it to Israel seven months later. It was taken to Kiriath-jearim, a few miles west of Jerusalem, where it stayed until David brought it to Jerusalem, his new capital.

The lack of political and military unity, which accounted for the loss of the Ark to the Philistines, was one of the major reasons for Israel's demand for a monarch. Samuel, released from his ministry to the priests at Shiloh since the day it was destroyed by the Philistines, had become an outstanding judge. In his old age he felt it was God's will to declare that God was purposing a new day—a monarchy should be established, replacing the clan rule by judges. So this called for a fresh reinterpretation of the covenant, showing the relevance of God's election of Israel for that time.

CHAPTER 4

The Davidic Covenant:
A New Covenant for Israel

DURING SAMUEL'S LAST YEARS as a circuit judge, a whole new era dawned on Israel. The period of the judges came to a close; the monarchy arose. In premonarchic days the Israelites were bound together by the religious ties of their twelve-tribe league. Their regular harvest festival pilgrimages to the shrine or tent which housed the Ark of the Covenant were times of renewal of the covenant and rededication to one another as members of the divinely elected people. Politically the people were disunited, having neither a political center nor a strong military force. Their leadership was dependent on the charismatic judges—men who arose in various tribes as leaders who had saved their people in some particularly evil time and event.

But the Canaanites had not been captured, even after the Israelites had lived a century in Canaan; and the Philistines, who came to Palestine in 1192 B.C., had by now captured many Hebrew villages. As noted in the previous chapter, they had even captured and destroyed the Israelites' central shrine at Shiloh and had taken the Ark of the Covenant (which they had captured at Aphek) with them, to their homeland.

Hence it was that venerable Samuel felt that a new age had come—the need of a monarch was now the desire of Yahweh himself. We read of Samuel's conviction in I Sam. 9:15-16: "Now the day before Saul came, the Lord had revealed to Samuel: 'Tomorrow about this time I will send to you a man from the land of Benjamin, and you shall

181

anoint him to be prince over my people Israel. He shall save my people from the hand of the Philistines.' " Thus the monarch is viewed as being a necessary instrument for the will of Yahweh in Israel's history—for it was through him that Yahweh would save his chosen people from extinction by the Philistines. Saul therefore, is anointed king. So Saul is more than a charismatic judge, he is the Messiah—the anointed—of Yahweh.

Unfortunately Saul's faith and actions did not fulfill Samuel's expectations, nor did he wage a successful war against the Canaanites. It was left to his successor David to rout the Philistines from the land. Theologically, we must move to David as the first real monarch, in whom the new era was to really begin. Centuries after David's reign, the people of Israel looked back to his rule as the ideal messianic relationship to Yahweh.

In recent years some Old Testament scholars have reversed their evaluation of II Sam. 7. Formerly they taught that it represented very late composition, and therefore had little to say about David. But some biblical scholars now believe that this passage is significant in the development of the messianic hope. It is now being suggested that this chapter was probably written in the days of King Solomon and was based on several short statements composed in the days of David. Since it is now believed to be of early origin, this passage, the so-called "prophecy of Nathan," is regarded very highly. We must therefore look at it closely, because it contains the basic elements of the Davidic covenant.

After David had been crowned king of Judah and Israel and had built a palace for himself in Jerusalem, the prophet Nathan pronounced a new relationship (covenant) between Yahweh and Israel. The former covenant, made between Israel and Yahweh at Sinai through Moses, was being superseded by a new covenant between Yahweh and David. Israel would still be the chosen people, but they would be led by a chosen dynasty—the Davidic dynasty.

Nathan's prophecy, reflecting earlier covenants, states:

"I have been with you wherever you went . . . and I will make for you a great name, like the name of the great ones of the earth" (II Sam. 7:9). The Lord promised David:

> I will give you rest from all your enemies. . . . I will raise up your son after you . . . and I will establish his kingdom. . . . I will be his father, and he shall be my son. . . . I will not take my steadfast love from him. . . . And your house [meaning descendants] and your kingdom shall be made sure for ever before me; your throne shall be established for ever" (II Sam. 7:11-16).

David immediately offered a prayer after hearing this prophecy from the lips of Nathan. His prayer included a recitation of God's saving acts in the past [1] similar to what he had heard as a boy at Shechem, Shiloh, or Bethel at the pilgrimage festivals (II Sam. 7:18-29). Thus, the Mosaic covenant undergirded David. 'There was no clean break with the past, yet a new and fresh reinterpretation of the concept of election took place.' The Davidic dynasty becomes the chosen channel through which God will act in the present and future in the historical life of Israel. (To be sure, at times on these pages we see some of the fingerprints of the Deuteronomic writer, who reedited this material after the Exile. This passage from II Samuel, however, does give us a feeling of authenticity from the time of the early Davidic dynasty.)

In order to see more clearly that the new order had been substituted for the old, let us observe some of the changes that were made. As we have noted, the charismatic leadership of the judges has now been taken over by the "anointed" of Yahweh. We note quite a difference in the conduct of warfare, for example, between the charismatic leadership of Gideon and the more rational leadership of the military genius, David. David ordered a census of his

---

[1] David's prayer was an expression of faith in what we call salvation-history (*Heilsgeschichte*; see page 1).

people so that he could know how many men he could count on in his military structure. He was condemned for having done so, for it suggested that he didn't really have faith in God to win his battles for him, regardless of numbers!

A new concept of government obviously came into being. Previously there had been no political unity. Israel's unity was based on her religious ties to Yahweh alone. Now a whole new set of government officers was established, including chief priests (Abiathar and Zadok) who were appointed by the head of the state. With new officers and state officials a new division of Israel was created—a division not based on tribal relationships but on administration. Furthermore, the new government had its first capital, not in a Judean or Israelite city but in a Canaanite city only recently captured —Jerusalem. With this new capital in Jerusalem went another new development: The new center for Israel now was political, not cultic. For the first time Israel was united by political ties.

With David's son, Solomon, a further new element entered the picture when he built his Temple in Jerusalem. For now Israel replaced the tent of meeting (which housed the Ark of the Covenant in the period of the judges) with a *house*. Furthermore, this Temple became a *national* Temple, inasmuch as the Ark of the Covenant was located in the Holy of Holies. The sacredness of Gilgal, Shiloh, and Shechem were now transferred to Jerusalem.

The duties of the priests changed at this time too. Formerly their task was threefold: to keep the shrine clean and ready for use; to proclaim oracles by use of the Urim and Thummim of their priestly "ephods" (arks); to instruct the laity in the laws of God and make necessary decisions concerning the Law when disputes arose. Now, with the Davidic dynasty, the priests gave fewer and fewer oracles by way of their Urim and Thummim. Instead, they substituted the office of official sacrificer, a task which the head of the family always had held previously. They continued as caretakers of the shrine and instructors of Torah (Law).

The king became responsible for the national Temple, so he subsidized its expenses. Previously, priests received their earnings through the gifts and sacrifices brought by the sacrificers. We can now understand a little better why King Josiah could order the people to institute the requirements of the Deuteronomic reform, 622 B.C.: 'the king was responsible not only for the Temple and its services but also for the religious life of the people! 'Yahweh had chosen the king as the channel through whom responsibility should flow. Little wonder that the prophets spoke directly to the king when religious matters were left untended.

The Egyptian beliefs regarding the relationship of the deity to the ruler may have influenced the coronation rites of David and his successors. Immediately after an Egyptian monarch was crowned, he was called a son of god. Thus the name Ramses means son of the sun, hence son of god. ("Ra" is an Egyptian god, the sun, and "-mses," a contraction of the Egyptian word "Moses," means "son.") The name Thutmoses means "son of Thut." But when Nathan quoted Yahweh as saying to David: "I will be his father, and he shall be my son" (II Sam. 7:14) he did not mean it biologically as was thought to be the case in Egypt. He was "adopted" as God's son.

Israel had conceived of the entire nation as being in this relationship—adopted by God—before the time of David. Now the monarch took this special role. Israel, however, was still conceived of as being a loved and chosen people and, by the later prophets, held in the father-son relationship.

As God's special representative, the king is also invested with responsibility for law and justice. In a sense he takes over, at least theoretically, some of the office of the priest, who was to instruct the laity in the Torah. The king actually delegated this authority to the priest who continued to instruct the laity. The king was responsible, however, for justice in the court and was especially concerned about the widow, the orphan, and the poor man before the courts.

Many psalms, some of which are quite ancient and reflect the early period of the monarchy, are shown as royal psalms. Some may have been used in the coronation services of the Davidic kings. Others were used in ceremonies where the king was the central figure. Some of these royal psalms are: Ps. 2, 18, 20, 21, 45, 72, 89, 101, 110, 132. In time, new annual festivals were developed, and these vied with the pilgrimage festivals for attendance. Some of the new annual festivals centered around David's bringing the Ark of the Covenant to Jerusalem. These psalms relate how Yahweh chose Zion (though a former Canaanite city) as his resting place. Ps. 132 shows the religious significance of Davidic coronations, how the assembly was called to worship, and the joy of receiving Yahweh's blessings. It is assumed that sacrifices were made too.

The place of Nathan should not be underestimated. His age was facing a religious crisis. He met it by reinterpreting the concept of God's election and showed how God had elected the Davidic dynasty as the means through which he would continue his saving actions in Israel's behalf.[1] Faith thus became relevant for a people who assumed that religion was a thing for their forefathers but not for them. David and his dynasty are now elevated to a position of significance almost equal to that of Moses. They are given tremendous responsibility as God's channels for his justice and responsibility for the instruction of his word.

In this new "theology of the dynasty" a truly wonderful concept developed, possibly in part through the theological insights of the historian who wrote down the life of David: God acts not only in historical and physical events, but also in the hearts of men. The days of miraculous intervention (as in the days of Moses, or the charismatic judges) were in their decline; God's activity is seen to be active in the subconscious, in the depths of motivations of men.[2]

---

[2] Note how Jer. 31:31-34 expanded this insight.

The story of Ahithophel points up this truth very well. Absalom, David's son, had started a rebellion, and King David had left the royal city of Jerusalem. David, the anointed of the Lord, prayed that Ahithophel, who had been his private counselor and who had turned to Absalom during the rebellion, would give counsel of foolishness (II Sam. 15:31). When Absalom asked for counsel of Ahithophel, he gave (without intending to) foolish counsel so that Absalom refused to abide by his advice. The writer inserts these theological convictions: "For the Lord had ordained to defeat the good counsel of Ahithophel, so that the Lord might bring evil upon Absalom" (II Sam. 17:14b). The point to observe is: God's saving action (in behalf of his anointed, David, who prayed) took place *in the heart* of Ahithophel—rather than moving in some physical event as was done at the crossing of the Reed Sea or the Jordan River.

A new concept of how God works was now developing: God works out his will in history through many media, one of which is in the everyday life of men, in the secular realm, wherever men are. Thus developed a whole new interest in the manner of the revelation of God's will. So we find in the writings of the history of David a great interest in psychological processes: hate and love, jealousy and pride. God's activities are viewed as including these areas through which his saving actions can be wrought.

So a new era was indeed born—a new kind of leadership, a new Davidic covenant, a new concept of a "house" for Yahweh, new religious festivals, and new psalms for bringing the Ark to Zion and for the coronation of the king. Indeed, there arose a fresh interpretation of the meaning of election and how God acts in the contemporary historical situation. The age of the monarchy was indeed an age of enlightenment. As we saw in Part II, the intellectual and spiritual life of Israel had been awakened.

CHAPTER 5

Prophecy and Deuteronomy

By THE TIME of Elijah (the middle of the ninth century
B.C.), Amos, Hosea, and Isaiah (the middle and close of
the eighth century B.C.), a new perspective had developed.
Formerly, Israel, the chosen seed, had looked forward to
the fulfillment of God's promises to the patriarchs. The
tribes looked forward to becoming a great people (which
they did in Egypt), to obtaining the promised land (which
Yahweh "gave" them through Joshua's conquests of
Canaan), and of being such a people that "all mankind
would be blessed" through them. Also, they had realized
another covenant: The dynasty of David had given them
a monarchy, military security, and justice. Now, however,
Israel looked back to that golden age of David, for fulfillment was a thing of the past. The perspective among the
vast majority of the laity (and perhaps the clergy too)
was backward, not forward. Festivals and worship centered
on praising Yahweh for what he had done for the fathers.
The assumption was that God was doing nothing in their
day. The question was: What is the relevance of the faith
of the fathers for today?

Nathan had shown the relevance of the faith by establishing a new covenant with the house of David. Elijah,
a century later, sought to clarify the meaning of Yahwism
for his day. Many of his people were worshiping the fertility and land deities. In fact, the worship of Yahweh
was in danger of being so compromised with Baalism
that the pure faith would be so diluted as to be unrecog-
nizable. Elijah's ("Yahweh is my God") voice therefore
called out: "Choose this day whom you will serve" (Josh.

24:15), giving the people a choice between Yahweh and Baal. The experiences on Mt. Carmel illustrated his prophetic demands for purification of the faith. His claim was that Yahweh, not Baal or Astarte, was in control of the seasons of fertilization of plants and animals.

The Eighth-Century Prophets

A century later, the great eighth-century prophets— Amos, Hosea, Isaiah, and Micah—dealt with the traditions that Yahweh was the God of Israel; had chosen (elected) them from among the nations; and had proved it by redeeming them from Egypt, giving them the land, and establishing the monarchy.

Each of the eighth-century prophets gave clear evidence of having known well the cultic creeds of their fathers, such as those in Josh. 24 and Deut. 26. Their vision was extended because they stood on the shoulders of those who went before them—the patriarchs, Moses, Joshua, the judges, David, and his outstanding prophet, Nathan. Undoubtedly they often had voiced their faith that Yahweh had heard the cry of their fathers when oppressed, and they recited how he had led them out of Egypt, had guided their steps in the wilderness, and had aided them in the conquest. God was known by his acts in the historical life of Israel.

Amos argued that this same God was still acting in *their* history. Faith therefore had a distinct relevance—for God was expecting specific fruits to issue from the life of both Judah and Israel (the northern kingdom). As a matter of fact, Yahweh was looking for justice, mercy, kindness, and compassion from *all* the nations, including Ammon, Moab, Philistia, Syria, Edom, and of course Judah and Israel (Amos 1–2).

The eighth-century prophets tried to show that Yahweh, whose covenant had been made with the fathers, expected loyalty of those of their day too. The backward look was good in the sense of having a feeling for God's acts in history, but the believers should also look to their own day. Where would Yahweh, the God of the oppressed, show his concerns today? Thus Amos lifted up some of the concerns which he felt were in the heart of God. He concluded that God was concerned that justice should prevail in the market-place (Amos 8:5), and should include the un-employed (Amos 8:6). Amos called the attention of Israel, who preferred to memorialize the past, to the fact that God looked to the present, and was concerned not so much with irreligion but with bad religion which was carried on in his name (Amos 2:7b-8; 2:12). Yahweh, deliverer from oppression, was concerned that

they [the unfeeling rich] trample the head of the poor into the dust of the earth,
    and turn aside from the way of the afflicted (Amos 2:7a).

Furthermore, justice could not be obtained at the courts because of bribery of the judges (Amos 5:12).

One of the truly great insights of Amos is his realization that God demands justice of all nations, not only of his chosen people. Wherever injustice, cruelty, inhumanity, or false religion exists,

the eyes of the Lord God are upon the sinful kingdom,
    and I will destroy it from the surface of the ground (Amos 9:8).

Yahweh's concerns for justice were not just for Israel and Judah, but for all nations, for whom he has always been responsible (Amos 9:7). When one reads Amos 1–2 in the light of Amos 9:8, he realizes that Yahweh is concerned with the history of all nations—not only with the history of Israel. God is the Lord of all history and of all nations. God is active in the movement of nations who migrate in order that they might find a land where they may fulfill their God-given destinies.

Much has been written about the prophets' attitude

toward the Temple, and its liturgy. At first glance, it seems
that the eighth-century prophets abrogated the sacrificial
system of Israel. But this is probably incorrect. It seems
more likely that they assumed that the sacrifices would
continue at the Temple, for these sacrifices and festivals
were *means* (not ends in themselves) by which and through
which men were able to realize that God had forgiven their
sins.

The prophetic concern about the sacrificial system was
that the *acts* of the worshiper should harmonize with the
life of the worshiper. Isaiah observed Judeans who lifted
up their hands to God in prayer even though those hands
had just signed foreclosure documents against widows and
orphans who were objects of God's concern. He therefore
cried out,

> Wash yourselves; make yourselves clean. . .
> cease to do evil,
>   learn to do good;
> seek justice,
>   correct oppression;
> defend the fatherless,
>   plead for the widow (Isa. 1:15-17).

Amos was concerned about those who came to worship
insincerely, hypocritically. He stated in God's behalf:

I hate, I despise your feasts,
  and I take no delight in your solemn assemblies
[such as our Christmases, and Easters?]. . . .
Take away from me the noise of your songs;
  to the melody of your harps I will not listen.
But let justice roll down like waters,
  and righteousness like an everflowing stream (Amos 5:21-24).

Here is a keen mind searching for the meaning and im-
plication of the covenant faith. In olden times—in the days
of Moses, Joshua, and the judges—a man's worship consisted
of reciting how God had saved the fathers at the Sea of

Reeds and how he had given them the Ten Commandments and the land. They were to obey the Ten Commandments; but, as we pointed out previously, these were negative statements—things which they should *not* do in order not to displease Yahweh.

Amos, Hosea, Isaiah, and Micah lifted up *affirmations* —stating clearly what God *does* want of Israel as an expression of gratitude for God's saving acts, namely: a moral life—justice in every walk of life. In the period of the judges the tribes were bound together by religious loyalties centered in their major shrine at Shiloh or Shechem. There were practically no political ties. The eighth-century prophets declared that Yahweh is concerned with how a man acts in his economic, political, domestic, international, as well as religious life.

Whereas Amos declared God's concern for justice, Hosea and Isaiah proclaimed the divine concern for trust and faithfulness, even as Joshua had declared it at Shechem (Josh. 24). God not only acted centuries before in behalf of Israel, they declared, but he was also acting in their own day. And his covenant was being broken by their unfaithfulness! Judah was acting like a "silly dove," flitting from embassy to embassy to find her security (Hos. 7:11). In giving gifts to various nations in exchange for national security, the people were playing the harlot—they were unfaithful to their marriage (covenantal partner) with Yahweh (Hos. 9:1-3).

Isaiah, following the insights of Hosea, who portrayed the love and pain of God when thwarted by his loved one, called for fidelity and trust. In speaking to Ahaz, who feared an invasion by Syria and Israel, Isaiah declared:

> If you will not believe,
>   surely you shall not be established
>   (Isa. 7:9*b*).

He called for expressions of loyalty and trust when he said:

In returning and rest you shall be saved;
  in quietness and in trust shall be your strength (Isa. 30:15).

Micah summed up the matter of the divine will for Judah when he declared that God wanted man to

do justice, and to love kindness
[*hesed,* steadfast love, loyalty to the covenant],
  and to walk humbly [trustfully] with your God (Mic. 6:8).

It seems obvious that there was no break with the covenant made with the fathers! For the people were to show their gratitude for his saving acts in their behalf by loving him and being obedient to his will. The prophets of the eighth-century spelled out in greater detail than had been done previously the positive expectations which the covenant entailed.

Against this background the revelation which Isaiah experienced (recorded in Isa. 6) and proclaimed to his contemporaries was the fact that the living God who spoke to Moses was still speaking in Isaiah's day—to those who were sensitive to his voice! Indeed, Isaiah experienced the "glory of the Lord," which Moses saw on Mt. Sinai and which led the people during their sojourn in the wilderness. Isaiah learned that "the whole earth [not just Mt. Sinai] is full of his [God's] glory" (Isa. 6:3). Those who thought Yahweh had spoken only to and for their forefathers found a new relevance for their faith and the meaning of their covenant when they heard the prophet declare: "Thus says the Lord." (Of course, though a man may see a new relevance to the traditional faith, it does not necessarily mean he admits nor adopts it. This was true in Isaiah's day.)

One of the extraordinary insights that came during the period was the new understanding of the way God spoke to his people. Previously God had spoken only to Moses and through Moses as his "mouthpiece" to the people. Later God had spoken through the charismatic judges and the priests with their sacred lots (Urim and Thummim). With the rise of prophecy, however, a new medium is opened for the divine revelation of Yahweh's will: the prophet received the "word" of God directly, not through another person (such as a priest or Moses). The prophet heard God with such personal inspiration that he declared to his audience: "Thus says the Lord." The prophet, filled with memories of the mighty acts of God in Israel's past, thought about the nature of God in view of these saving acts.

Thus, the prophets inferred from God's acts in their behalf that the nature of God included the attributes of justice, love, mercy, compassion, and holiness. Believing that God was the only living God, and that his attributes were justice, compassion, and mercy, the prophets rethought and reexperienced the faith of their fathers and found the living God to be the Lord of history of *all* time, including their own. This Lord of history had a message for their day which they learned partly by inference from the past events through which God acted in Israel's history and partly from awareness of his presence and will. This they declared to their contemporaries. Thus, the God who acts became known as the God who *speaks*, and his message was declared by the prophet who prefaced his oracles with the words: "Thus says the Lord."

It was toward the close of the next century (the seventh century B.C.) that another medium was developed for revealing the will of God, namely the written word. The core of the book of Deuteronomy has the honor of being known as the first book in history to be declared the "Word of God." We turn to it now.

The Book of Deuteronomy

When the writer of Deuteronomy wrote, no new "saving act" had occurred since the days of David. Many concluded therefore that the days of Yahweh's activity and concern had ceased. But the eighth-century prophets (Amos, Hosea, Isaiah, Micah) bore witness to the divine concern for his chosen people. In fact, God had a "word" for them, as we observed above.

Though the heart of the book of Deuteronomy was found in the Temple about 621 B.C., in the days of King Josiah, large portions of it were probably written several decades before that time. Some scholars are convinced that much of Deuteronomy was written in the northern kingdom by Levites who went about the land preaching. If so, many of their sermons may be incorporated into what we now call Deuteronomy. The twelve sermonettes were combined with some legal codes into the literary form of a sermon, a farewell sermon by Moses in Moab. The book is definitely a reinterpretation of the ancient traditions of God's saving acts in history in an attempt to make them relevant for the new age, the latter part of the seventh century B.C.

It is illuminating to observe that Deuteronomy is not interested in the monarchy—though Josiah is king. II Kings 22–23 tells us how Josiah joined in supporting the religious reforms called for in the newly discovered scroll which had been proclaimed the "Word of God" by the prophetess Huldah. One provision of these religious reforms was that henceforth all worship was to be centralized in one place, instead of at the various shrines over the countryside which had been used for local worship. (We cannot help but wonder how much the enforcement of this provision may have been motivated by political reasons as far as the youthful king, Josiah, was concerned. The reform required all his subjects to come to his capital, Jerusalem, for pilgrimages three times a year.)

Deuteronomy is an interesting admixture of prophetic and priestly concepts. The prophetic concern to love God and do justly is caught up in the demands for loyalty to the sacrificial cult. The demand for loyalty finds its roots in the past—in the covenant made with Moses and the fathers at Sinai. Israel, not the Davidic dynasty, is very definitely the chosen vehicle through which God is to work.

The task of Deuteronomy was not to develop new traditions, nor to add to the old traditions new concepts, nor to enlarge them in any way. Its task was like that of a preacher, one of explanation or interpretation. It interpreted the traditions of God's saving acts in the contemporary historical life of the nation.

Deuteronomy is retrospective. It seeks to draw people back to the "good old days" of the traditions. The fact that it has no good word for the monarchy suggests that those who wrote the book felt that the monarchy was an aberration and not the desire of Yahweh. The monarchy had, in a sense, replaced Yahweh as king, lawgiver, and ruler. Hosea held this position (see Hos. 4). Samuel and some of the prophets, such as Isaiah, assumed that the monarchy was a divine office, and even dreamed of a wonderful future when the "anointed" would bring peace to the world.

At first Jeremiah gave strong support to the Deuteronomic reform. Later he realized that goodness and faith could not be legislated, and he foresaw the need for a new covenant (Jer. 31:31). He was later joined by the prophetic voices of Ezekiel and Second Isaiah (Isa. 40–55) who foresaw a new era ahead based on a new saving act of God.

The Deuteronomic reform apparently did not last long. It seems to have come to a stop when Josiah was killed at Megiddo by Pharaoh Neco of Egypt (about 609 B.C.).

Though the reform movement was short-lived, the importance of the book lived on for centuries. That is because of the affirmation that Deuteronomy was "the Word of the Lord." When men wanted to know the will of God, they were told to look it up in the book! Thus the idea of inspired scripture knelled the death of prophecy. Instead of inquiring of a prophet, "What says the Lord," men now went to a book to ask: "What does the written word say?" This ultimately gave rise to the legalism of the

Pharisees, who sought to be obedient to the total law of God.

The author of Deuteronomy was deeply concerned about making faith relevant to his contemporaries. Read Deut. 5:1-5, and observe how men of a much later period than that of Moses were to say: "Not with our fathers did the Lord make this covenant, but with us, who are all of us here alive this day." As each man and family affirmed the covenant for himself, he identified himself with his forefathers to whom the original covenant was made. Even today the modern man of Judaism states at the *seder* (Passover meal) that God rescued "me" and delivered "me" from Egypt and the Sea of Reeds!

CHAPTER 6

Prophecies of a New
Saving Act of God

NEBUCHADNEZZAR TOOK Judah captive twice within a decade, first in 597, then 587 B.C. After the last captivity Nebuchadnezzar totally destroyed the city of Jerusalem, including Solomon's Temple. Priests carried the sacred vessels to Babylon as booty for the conquering king. We have seen how the people wept by the waters of Babylon as they trudged as slaves into a foreign and "unclean" land.

In Babylon they could no longer offer their sacrifices, for Deuteronomy had established but one place for sacrifice, Jerusalem. But the exiles could gather and recall the great events they had known and loved on Mt. Zion. Little wonder that they dreamed and yearned for the hills of Mt. Zion, where God had tabernacled with his people in Solomon's Temple.

But the exiles had to wait till the coming of the Persian, Cyrus the Great, in 538 B.C., before they could return to their native land. By that time, the boys who had gone into captivity were now sixty-five to seventy-five years old; but the children had listened night after night to the glories of Jerusalem and the lore of the Temple and its rituals. They also had heard of the words of Jeremiah which foretold their exile and the reasons why it would be so. They read into the events of their national catastrophe the claims of faith: Their exile was the judgment of God upon them for having refused to be obedient to the covenant. God did not force them to keep the covenant; yet they, though free to keep or break the covenant, denied it and consequently reaped the whirlwind. Their lives, as Joshua had proclaimed (Josh. 24:20), were cursed.

This philosophy (or theology) of history was an outgrowth of the prophetic understanding of history as Amos proclaimed it. Reread Amos 1–2 carefully. List those things which God is against, such as cruelty. And then list what God must be striving for among the nations. The plan seems clear: God is searching for a nation (s) who will live with justice, righteousness, compassion, honor, and godliness. Those who refuse it will feel the brunt of war—for nations whose national policies are based on cruelty, inhumanity, greed, jealousy, dishonor, and bad religion, as portrayed in Amos 1–2, are doomed to international conflict. Peace is impossible; war, inevitable. And war is thus seen as the fruit of immorality, the judgment of God.

Some unknown priests in Babylon during the exile spent a great deal of time working with the histories (J and E or JE) of Judah and Israel. They were not so much concerned with writing a simple narrative of the events as they were of writing an account which would illustrate the theology of history which they had formulated, based on the teachings of Amos and Isaiah. They edited, or compiled, the accounts which we know as the books of Deuteronomy, Joshua, Judges, I and II Samuel, I and II Kings. In their compilation these priests chose to include those events which best illustrated their religious convictions.

These convictions may be stated as a fourfold philosophy of history: (a) Israel sinned; (b) she was punished; (c) she repented; (d) she was delivered (see Judg. 2:18-19). Each judge in the book of Judges and each king (especially those from the northern kingdom, Israel) received a Deuteronomic judgment concerning their lives (for example, I Kings 14:21-24). If they served other gods or worshiped at other shrines rather than at Jerusalem, they sinned and brought evil consequences to their people. Repentance was required to reestablish right relationships with their covenant partner.

The Priest-Prophet, Ezekiel, Foresees a New Age

Ezekiel, who had been a priest in Jerusalem at the time of the captivity in 597 B.C., was one of those exiled to Babylonia. He knew the pain of forced travel and the humiliation of carrying the sacred vessels of the Temple to a new land to be displayed as trophies of war. Though in exile, he followed closely the activities in Jerusalem for many years and saw clearly that Jerusalem and Judah were doomed because of their immorality. He used many methods in his ministry to get his message across—but to little avail. People loved to hear him preach because he had such a lovely voice; so he refused to preach. He turned to the use of allegory (Ezek. 23 and 24) and symbolic prophecy (Ezek. 4), but in vain. He was finally convinced that the glory of the Lord that had come to Jerusalem and to Solomon's Temple had departed!

It was not till many years later, in Babylonia, that Ezekiel changed his ministry from prophecies of judgment to prophecies of hope. His vision of the "valley of dry bones" (Ezek. 37) changed his message. He was convinced that God was going to act anew in Israel's behalf, even as he had done for the slaves in Egypt. The people were saying: "Our bones are dried up, and our hope is lost; we are clean cut off" (Ezek. 37:11). Ezekiel had a vision of the life-giving "breath [spirit] of God" [1] moving upon his exiled people. The promise was given: "I will put my Spirit within you, and you shall live, and I will place you in your own land; then you shall know that I, the Lord, have spoken, and I have done it, says the Lord" (Ezek. 37:14). Christians today are still inspired to sing: "Breathe on me, Breath of God."

Ezekiel was convinced that a new saving action of God was about to take place, a new baptism, a new covenant.[2]

---

[1] Compare with Gen. 2:7 (J): "Then the Lord . . . breathed into his nostrils the breath of life; and man became a living being."

[2] See Ezek. 36:25-28.

The old covenant was giving way for a new covenant—a new deliverance was being planned by the mind of God. This deliverance, as with the Mosaic deliverance, was not because of the merits of Israel but because of the grace of God alone: "For the sake of my holy name, which you have profaned" (Ezek. 36:22). Because Yahweh is the kind of God that he is, he will redeem his people in oppression in Babylonia.

The prophet saw a renewal of life, a cleansing and refreshing action on God's part toward Israel: "I will sprinkle clean water upon you, and you shall be clean. . . . A new heart I will give you, and a new spirit I will put within you; and I will take out of your flesh the heart of stone and give you a heart of flesh" (Ezek. 36:25-26). Believing that Yahweh was the same God throughout the centuries, Ezekiel sought to make the faith of the fathers relevant for his own age.

This hope of restoration arose out of a twofold source: First, Ezekiel was steeped in the religious traditions of his people; he believed that Yahweh had redeemed them in Egypt, delivered them at the Sea of Reeds, provided food (manna) and the ten "words" at Sinai, protected and guided them in the wilderness, and finally given them the land of Canaan. Besides this confidence in the Lord who acted in the historical life of Israel, Ezekiel had also experienced the presence of Yahweh and was convinced that God was still concerned about the welfare of his people. Ezekiel's religious experience is described in poetic form in the first two chapters of his book. He likened God unto light, yet one who is very personal—so personal that he commissioned Ezekiel to a specific task in behalf of Israel (Ezek. 2:1-9). The last eight chapters of Ezekiel were written out of the conviction that the New Jerusalem would be built with the Temple as its center, with all life finding its purposes in the central place of worship in Zion. Ezekiel was confident that God was ready to lead his people back home.

Isaiah of Babylon, Prophet of a New Covenant

About this time another great man, an unknown prophet-singer, whom for lack of name we may call Isaiah of Babylon, or Second Isaiah, wrote the passages found in Isa. 40–55. From both a literary and a religious viewpoint his writings are among the most elevated and influential in the entire Old Testament.

In a letter to the exiles in Babylon shortly after 586 B.C. Jeremiah had stated that they should settle down, marry, beget children, and pray for the welfare of their city; and that after seventy years they would then be permitted to return. Isaiah of Babylon, writing about 540 B.C., was convinced that "the days of their warfare were accomplished." He called the exiles to prepare for a grand and new Exodus far beyond what Moses and the slaves had witnessed in Egypt—a return to the promised land.

Here is something entirely new. Isaiah of Babylon is not reciting the confessional ritual of the traditions. On the contrary, he is saying new traditions will be developed. God will do a "new thing." A new and more glorious salvation is ahead for Israel—greater than that of the deliverance in Egypt! Isaiah of Babylon rhapsodizes about a new Exodus, wherein the Lord will make a highway from Babylon to Jerusalem, making the mountains to be brought low, the valleys to be exalted (lifted up to meet the lowered mountains), the crooked made straight and the rough places smooth and plain (Isa. 40:1-4).

The old encounter of Yahweh with Moses will be far surpassed, because, in this fresh and *new* Exodus, the

glory of the Lord shall be revealed,
   and all flesh [all peoples of all nations] shall see it together,
  for the mouth of the Lord has spoken (Isa. 40:5).

The return will be as gentle as that of a shepherd leading his flock:

> He will feed his flock like a shepherd,
>   he will gather the lambs in his arms,
> he will carry them in his bosom,
>   and gently lead those that are with young (Isa. 40:11).

A new outburst of kindness and of renewal will be released by Yahweh upon his beloved ones. An entirely new field of divine action is to be opened up, an entirely *new* salvation: a *new* covenant, a *new* Exodus, a *new* David, a *new* Word—an entirely *new* thing! This *new* salvation is in discontinuity with the old. God is working something entirely *new* for these *new* days.

Deuteronomy was a kind of reformation theology—it looked back to what had been. Isaiah of Babylon, Ezekiel, and Jeremiah looked toward an entirely new encounter that would give a new heart, a new spirit, a new cleansing, a new hope, a new life! Out of the judgment that the people of Israel had endured as a consequence of their infidelity, a new beginning was being offered them.

The source for this faith was not so much in God's *acts* in history as the "Word" of God which "will stand for ever" (Isa. 40:8). It was not that Israel's sense of past history was overlooked, for this would be to misread the prophet, but that her hope was vested in "the Word" spoken in history.

It is well to remember that in the century we are discussing—the sixth century B.C.—a basic question was being asked in many countries of the world: What is it that never changes amidst all the changes of life? Buddha of India, Confucius of China, Zoroaster of Persia, the Eleatic philosophers of Asia Minor were giving their answer. The philosophers were suggesting: water, air, or Being. Isaiah of Babylon admitted that all things change—grass withers, the flower fades. Even people, like grass, fade away, but "the word of our God will stand for ever!"

The new covenant very definitely is related to Israel's opportunity to help all mankind to come into a vital, living, relationship with God. Isaiah of Babylon says:

> I am the Lord, I have called you in righteousness,
>   I have taken you by the hand and kept you;
> I have given you as a covenant to the people,
>   a light to the nations,
>   to open the eyes that are blind,
> to bring out the prisoners from the dungeon,
>   from the prison those who sit in darkness,
> I am the Lord, that is my name (Isaiah 42:6-8*a*).

In order to win others to the love of God, Israel must become a suffering servant. Here is a *new* Israel! Not a warrior people but one of justice, humility, deep sensitivity (Isa. 42:1-4; 53:1-12). Here we see a vision of true greatness—the greatness of God himself. We see God's method of winning others to himself—the way of suffering, vicarious suffering. (When Israel, as a people, refused to accept this great opportunity, she rejected the hour of her greatness. It was for Jesus of Nazareth, one of Israel's sons, the suffering servant of God, to come and to carry the cross which Israel refused. The church is commissioned to carry his cross in our time.)

Here then is a new conception of the old tradition concerning election. Continuity of the covenant is now seen to be dependent on a person's response, rather than being based on the sonship of Abraham. Continuity of the covenantal relationship includes the matter of acceptance of obligation toward other nations. It is not a matter of achieving a place in the sun, nor of sitting at the right hand of God in military power and authority. It is an opportunity of helping pagans, who spend countless hours in searching for meaning and purpose, to find the way to life! The chosen are to be a priesthood to all the nations of the earth. Here is the seed of the Protestant doctrine of the priesthood of all believers—man (each person of the covenant community) is a priest to his neighbor. Priesthood means more than direct access to God; it means primarily responsibility for one's neighbor, that he (or she) may come to know God and his will for his life.

CHAPTER 7

The Postexilic Response

ONE OF THE GREAT tragedies in history occurred when Israel refused to seize her opportunity as enunciated by Second Isaiah. True, a small number of Israelites returned to Jerusalem and Judah shortly after the days of Cyrus' decree (after 538 B.C.), but those who returned were not dedicated to the great vision of Second Isaiah. They did not perceive themselves as a "light to the nations," as having a priestly function to all mankind. They were concerned with reestablishing the cult at the Temple in Jerusalem, with its rituals, festivals, and sacrifices. They kept the shell but lost the kernel of their faith. They even looked for an "anointed one" (messiah) in Zerubbabel the governor of Judah in the days of Haggai and Zechariah; but it was a short-lived hope! Although we do not know what happened to Zerubbabel, we do know that the theology of the throne (the Davidic covenant) did not prosper.

In the decades following the great insights of Second Isaiah and the return to Jerusalem of a small percentage of those who had lived in exile, the faith of the Jews in their homeland, Judah, languished. There were a few prophets—Haggai, Zechariah, and Malachi—but their successes were limited mostly to rebuilding the Temple on a very small scale—it was probably little more than a shanty! There were also very capable writers (such as the authors of the Priestly Code, Chronicles, and Ezra and Nehemiah), but these writers looked backward, not forward. They were all too concerned with what God had done in the past and not concerned enough with what God was doing or was going to do in their day. Nonetheless, they were concerned

205

with making their faith relevant for their age, as we shall now see by turning to their writings.

The Priestly Code

The writer of the Priestly Code was convinced that Yahweh had elected Israel as his special, chosen people. His document was an attempt to show the divine origin of these chosen people, and especially the origin of their sacred institutions, such as the rite of circumcision; observance of the Sabbath; and the laws governing sacrifices, rituals, and festivals. All of these had been revealed, according to the writer of the Priestly Code, to Moses at Sinai. The writer's basic aim was to show how the only existing God became the sovereign of Israel. To do this he developed the idea of a theocracy.

The theocracy was not the government of the state under the immediate direction of God. It was a religious community, a "holy" nation, a kind of "church" within the Persian empire. Though Persia controlled Judah politically, the religious community developed a new kingdom within the Persian kingdom—a kingdom of God! The writer's aim was to show that the one transcendent God, the invisible sovereign of the world, was the God of Israel, who had, in fact, chosen Israel as a distinctive people. To do this the writer developed the concept of a theocracy based on these elements: the sovereign (God), his subjects (Israel), his land (Canaan, which he gave to Israel), and his tithes (the financial support for his kingdom, paid by his subjects).

Our interest in this section is in the theological understanding of this writer of the Priestly Code and his reinterpretation of the Mosaic covenant in an attempt to make the faith relevant for his age. The author of the Priestly Code does not include the Davidic covenant. Apparently he considered the monarchy an evil institution. We have seen in Part II that the systematic arrangement of his material is classified under four basic periods, and each division is headed by a man through whom God had revealed his will under unique circumstances—Adam, Noah, Abraham, and Moses.

A key statement in understanding this writer's theology is found in Gen. 17:1, a passage where God is speaking to Abram: "I am God Almighty; walk before me, and be blameless." God's desire is not for sacrifices *per se,* but for a blameless (perfect) man. Caught up in this phrase are the moral categories of Micah: to do justly, love mercy, and trustingly walk in the presence of God (Mic. 6:8). Here we see more than a series of negative commandments, as in the Mosaic decalogue. There is a positive affirmation of what God does want of a man.

The covenant is thus made relevant for the fifth century B.C. by restating the covenants to Abraham and Moses in positive terms needed in his day. Man is able to be "blameless" by being obedient to the many rules which the divine sovereign gave at Sinai concerning sacrifices, rituals, and festivals. So the ideal of a blameless life is tied up with the priestly concern for the cult and its rituals.

The influence of both Second Isaiah and Ezekiel are seen in the Priestly Code. For example, at the time of the destruction of Jerusalem Ezekiel had prophesied that the Glory of the Lord (that is, God himself) had left the Temple because of the sins of Judah. Sometime after the exile of 587 B.C. Ezekiel prophesied that the Glory of the Lord would return to Judah. Ezek. 40–48 is the soil from which the roots of the priestly code grow. His priestly concerns for the Temple as the center of the life of God's people are frequently evident. Following the teachings of Ezek. 43:7-9, which states that God will "dwell in the midst of the people of Israel," the priestly writer (P) assumes that the sovereign God has returned to Zion and that all may return to Jerusalem to witness the "glory of the Lord."

The influence of Second Isaiah on the priestly group is seen in the story of creation found in Gen. 1:1–2:4a. Second Isaiah had stated: "The word of our God will stand for ever" (Isa. 40:8b). Furthermore, the earth and all its inhabitants were created by the "Word." The first chapter of Genesis (P) assumes that the creative Word orders the creation of the world. God himself did not fashion it, as an artificer might do, nor was it formed in accordance with Babylonian myths which the erudite writer knew, but the world was created at the word of God!

The priestly writer conceived that Israel could be in the Persian world, but not of it. That is, the *real* kingdom was the kingdom of God; God alone was Israel's true sovereign, even though his subjects paid taxes to a political ruler. Here is the basis for much of Christian thinking of later years—that we can be in the world, but not of the world.

What a change or reinterpretation of the covenants has taken place. The Davidic covenant, with its accent on the political obligations, and its emphasis on being in and of this world, has been laid aside! The emphasis now is on the Mosaic covenant and particularly on the revelations made to Moses at Sinai. Interest now is on ritual, sacrifice, and festivals, described in Exod. 34:29–40:38, Num. 1:1–10:28, and Leviticus. Here the political aspects are insignificant.

When the priestly writer wrote this brief but marvelous work, he was in Babylon, though no longer in enforced exile. He had voluntarily remained. He wrote in an age when the Babylonians worshiped great stone images of their gods and when his fellow Israelites felt that their faith must not be very relevant for their days in Babylon! The writer's remarkable concept of the Creative Word, the transcendent God, the Sovereign of the Universe, who had chosen Israel as his people, inspired many of his fellows to return to God. Many apparently returned to Judah under the leadership of Ezra (and possibly of Nehemiah, though he may have come before the Priestly Code was written). Even so, his work has the "backward" look, for it looks to the past for the golden age when Abraham and Moses revealed God's will for his subjects. We can imagine that his message was a great inspiration to the Jews, formerly exiles in Babylon, who had settled in this "unclean" land, yet wanted to worship Yahweh as their God. Inasmuch as the emphasis is on the sacrifices of the Temple, there is an unwritten call to all the Jews living away from the homeland to return.

Nehemiah, Ezra, and the Chronicler

Both Nehemiah (who went to Judah about 444 B.C.) and Ezra (about 397 B.C.) represent purist radicals. To make their faith relevant, these purists codified the covenant, making the "gift" of Sinai a legal system. The elected of God were now to be obedient to the *Law*.

It is interesting to observe that a century after the time of Second Isaiah, about 540 B.C., there were still many Jews in Babylon—enough so that Nehemiah, and later Ezra, could lead groups back to Jerusalem. Obviously the great return expected by Second Isaiah had not materialized.

Nehemiah, though interested in the political issues, demanded reforms in the cult and in the community itself. He excluded all aliens from worship in Jerusalem and dissolved all marriages of those who had married non-Jewish partners (Neh. 13:1-3; 23-28). He also demanded strict regulation of the offerings at the Temple (Neh. 13:10-13), ordered strict observance of the Sabbath (Neh. 13:15-23), and purged the Temple of improper use by outsiders (Neh. 13:4-9).

Nehemiah's critical and negative work was augmented by the more positive approach of Ezra. Ezra, who also came from Babylon, was—like Nehemiah—a man with governmental credentials. As we noted in Part I, he was appointed by the Persian king to be secretary of religious affairs in Judah. With this authority he descended on Judah with considerable power and prestige. He too was a racial purist. But he had something Nehemiah had not had: a book of the Law. Scholars are divided as to what that book was, though they are agreed that it contained much of the legal section of the Pentateuch. It possibly included the last chapters of Exodus, Leviticus, and first ten chapters of Numbers.

Ezra came with the intent of reviving the faith for his generation in Judea. His task was to reinterpret the concepts of election and the covenant. He, following Deuteronomy and the Priestly Code, based his work on reorganizing the cultic community. The major event of his work was the renewal of the covenant, which took place at the reading of the Book of Law before all Israel. This public reading was reminiscent of the Shechem festivals (Josh. 24), for it required all the congregation to renew their pledge of allegiance (their covenant) to Yahweh.

Whether or not Ezra actually presented the Priestly Code at this time we do not know. It was about this time (400 B.C. or shortly thereafter), however, that the Pentateuch was accepted as scripture, giving Judah five inspired books (scrolls) which contained the word of God. Formerly they had only Deuteronomy. Added now to it were the books we know as Genesis, Exodus, Leviticus, and Numbers. What had been considered more as a "gift" of life and the media for right relationships between Yahweh and his people now became a matter of Law. Other scholars believe that the "Law" which Ezra read to the Jews in Judah may well have been the Pentateuch, the first five books of the Old Testament. (This seems likely.)

With Ezra Judaism was born. The question before good Jews from now on was: Have you been obedient to the Law? Interest in statehood seemed to disappear, and in its place rose a deep passion for obedience to the divine sovereign of their theocracy. As seen in our study of the Priestly Code, the religious community became a kind of church within the empire—in the world, but not of the world.

The relevance of faith for this new age turned not upon

how God had revealed himself in nature or even supremely in their history but upon the Law. Legalism had set in. Instead of the Ten Commandments serving Israel, Israel became subservient to the Law. (Jesus was to ask which was right: Is man to serve the Law, or the Law serve man?)

An entirely new element entered the life of Israel: Whereas Israel once looked upon the will of Yahweh as personal and active in history (both the past and the present), she now looked upon the will of Yahweh as something fixed and beyond time (that is, beyond and above history). The faith in the saving acts of God in contemporary history was gone, and in its place was an emphasis upon obedience to the written and unwritten law. Thus Judaism was born, with its concern for the punctilious observance of every law.

About 300 B.C., the Chronicler (author of I and II Chronicles) wrote a history of Israel and carried it down to the time of Nehemiah. His theology shows close kinship to the writer of the Priestly Code, who was his spiritual mentor. The Chronicler, however, was a much inferior thinker and made no new contributions in his attempts to reinterpret the faith.

The Chronicler's interests were centered in the Temple and its rituals. He greatly appreciated the levitical choirs, which he considered to have originated with David.[1] His basic aim was a deeply spiritual one based on the interpretations of the Priestly Code, namely, that the theocracy was founded by God through Moses and that it continued without a break down to the time of Nehemiah.

The Chronicler makes a great case for the Davidic covenant. He loved David so much that he deleted all stories which showed him to have been a man with evil passions. It is evident that the Chronicler had a strong interest in the Messiah, with the Davidic covenant in the golden age of Israel's past as his ideal.

---

[1] The orchestras, choral groups, and most of the rituals he described were certainly of the fourth century B.C., rather than those of the monarchy.

Ruth and Jonah

The book of Ruth was written by a man who was theologically and socially incensed against the exclusivism of his day. Nehemiah and Ezra had denounced all marriages of Jews with foreigners (non-Jews). In fact, Ezra had issued a decree that all male Jews be divorced from their foreign wives (Ezra 10:2-5). From this time forward the emphasis on membership in the Jewish community of faith was a matter of one's birth. This meant, from a practical standpoint, that every male considered it very important to be able to trace his ancestry to a Jewish father, grandfather, great-grandfather, and so forth.

The book of Ruth was written, in part, to contradict this attitude of exclusiveness. The story tells how Naomi, a native of Bethlehem, returned to Bethlehem after the death of her husband and two sons in Moab. Ruth, her Moabite daughter-in-law, returned with her. Since Naomi had no children, she was greatly concerned about restoring her family line (Ruth 1:11-13). Ruth, a foreigner, came to her aid by marrying Boaz. To them was born Obed, who was to become the grandfather of David. Thus a foreign woman, a Moabite, was used of God to restore the family line of Naomi. Not only so, but Ruth the foreigner was well accepted by Judeans who never once questioned her status as wife to Boaz. The story of Ruth clearly indicated that children of mixed marriages could be blessed of God; for did not the great King David trace his ancestry back to such a mixed marriage?

God's methods of electing his "chosen people" were not biological ones, nor national, nor racial ones, but spiritual!

The message of Jonah also attempted to contradict the theology of racism. This book shows that God is interested not in the descendants of Abraham alone but in all mankind—even in the most hated enemy of Israel, Nineveh! God's love embraces men of all nations—a fact which the Jews of this period did not appreciate! But the writer of the short story Jonah made a great theological contribution to all time: The doctrine of election is not based on race, it is based on God's love for his creature, man; it is God's will that all men turn to him, acknowledge his sovereignty, express gratitude for his providence and love, and choose to be obedient to those ways which lead to life and peace.

The Spiritualization of the Cult

One of the great theological contributions of the post-exilic period was the realization that the individual could have a personal relationship with Yahweh. Formerly it was thought that the individual was more or less lost in the collective life of the community—in other words if the community repented, the individual was "saved"; if the community sinned and refused to repent, the individual was caught in the collective judgment. A new theological insight into the significant place of the individual was now recognized, however, and came to expression especially in Ezekiel and in Psalms.

Ezekiel took issue with a favorite, though pessimistic, proverb of his day: "The fathers have eaten sour grapes, and the children's teeth are set on edge" (Ezek. 18:2). He disagreed with Deuteronomy which argued that the children, unto the third and fourth generation, were to be punished for their fathers' sins. In disagreeing with this theology, Ezekiel pointed out that each man is punished for his own sin, and each man is saved by his own decisions and actions. Ezekiel interpreted the "religious" man as one who was saved not by good works but by having decided for Yahweh! Because of his decision for Yahweh, the religious man desired to be obedient, and, hence, obeyed the laws of God. His obedience was a sign of his commitment, not an expression of being saved by good works! Ezekiel challenged the men of his day to realize that God's covenant with the Judeans was based not on their being heirs of Abraham, but on their decision to accept God and to acknowledge the divine claims upon their lives. He also pointed out that Yahweh did not desire that men should die; rather he desired that they should live. At this point he sounds like Amos: "Seek good . . . that you may live" (Amos 5:14a).

This emphasis on the significance of the individual's decision to acknowledge God and accept his laws is basic to understanding what is meant by the "spiritualization of the cult." The emphasis is not on acts of worship but on the life of the worshiper. The rites, sacrifices, and festivals are not abrogated, but point toward inner and personal meaning. The psalmists began to move toward the inner meaning of the cultic activities too. Thus we have such a significant phrase as:

> Let my prayer be counted as incense before thee,
> and the lifting up of my hands as an evening sacrifice.
>
> (Ps. 141:2)

The inner life of prayer is seen as even more vital than the act of burning incense, and the lifting up of hands to God in prayer as more meaningful than offering sacrifices.

Such phrases as "circumcise your hearts" (Deut. 10:16; Lev. 26:41; Jer. 4:4) clearly refer to the importance of the inner life of the worshipers. Stephen's sermon angered the Sanhedrin because he identified his hearers with the "uncircumcised in heart and ears" who "resist the Holy Spirit" (Acts 7:51). This spiritualization of the cult is a significant reinterpretation of man's relationship to God. It puts the basis of God's electing his people on an entirely different basis. God gives man some responsibility in this matter of election, namely, that he must resist his stubbornness, he must "will" to receive the mark of sonship placed upon his spirit—he must "circumcise his heart"—these are the prerequisites to God's action.

Though such ideas as circumcision of the heart, prayer as

sacrifice, and prayer as incense pointed toward the personal and inner life of the worshiper, they did not necessarily point away from the physical acts of worship. At first, those who sought inner meaning and inner confirmation continued to observe the rules governing the acts of worship. They were circumcised, observed the temple sacrifices, and festivals as required by the law. Nonetheless, the seed was sown for a new view of the cult, especially concerning blood sacrifices:

> Sacrifice and offering thou dost not desire;
>   but thou hast given me an open ear.
> Burnt offering and sin offering
>   thou hast not required. . . .
> I delight to do thy will, O my God;
>   thy law is within my heart (Ps. 40:6, 8).

Ps. 50:8 declares categorically:

> I will accept no bull from your house,
>   nor he-goat from your folds.

From this desire for personal relationships with God and a lessening of interest in the sacrificial system, the day came when the pious man found his greatest values in life in pure contemplation of and in communion with Yahweh:

> And there is nothing upon earth that I desire besides thee.
> My flesh and my heart may fail,
>   but God is the strength of my heart and my portion for ever
> (Ps. 73:25b-26).

The psalmist declared his high evaluation of communion with God when he declared "thy steadfast love is better than life" (Ps. 63:3). More valuable than festivals, or rituals, or burnt offerings, and perhaps even than recitals of God's saving acts in the past, is the present awareness of God's steadfast love! We begin to feel the great passion of those whose life is caught up in the mystery of God's great love: "For God so loved the world . . . ." To know this as a fact for one's life is sweeter than all other religious claims or acts of worship.

The stage is set for a fresh interpretation of the meaning of God's election of his people, what election presupposes, what is expected of those whom he elects, and what it means to be in a right (covenantal) relationship with God. To this concern Jesus, Peter, and Paul addressed themselves. With the advent of Jesus and his apostles we hear of a new Israel, a new covenant, a fresh outburst of love from God which brought a new Exodus for oppressed man.

Epilogue

The Value of the Old Testament for Christians

THE OLD TESTAMENT is of value to persons whose interests are in many diverse disciplines. Let us illustrate this briefly. Persons who love great literature will value the Old Testament highly because it contains some of the best literature ever penned by man. We have previously noted Carlyle's judgment that the book of Job is "one of the grandest things ever written with the pen." The book of Ruth is considered to be one of the finest short stories in all literature. The poetry of the Old Testament contains outstanding love songs, odes, hymns, laments, monologues, dialogues, and affirmations of faith. Proverbs, history, and drama find their place too. From a literary point of view, the Old Testament is a treasure house of books of rare literary value.

For those whose intellectual discipline is centered in law, the Old Testament offers knowledge of some of the earliest codes of law of civilized man. Of special interest are the Covenant Code (Exod. 20:22–23:19); the Ritual Decalogue (Exod. 34:10-26); the Twelve Curses (Deut. 27:14-26); the Ten Commandments (Deut. 5:6-21, Exod. 20:1-17); the Deuteronomic Code (Deut. 12–26); the Holiness Code (Lev. 17–26); and the Priestly Code (note especially the legal sections in Leviticus, Exodus, and Numbers). Their interests would be heightened by clear differentiation between two basic types of law, casuistry (laws which begin with "if . . .") and apodictic (unconditional laws as in Ten Commandments). Both reflect knowledge of ancient

legal systems long before the time of Moses. Yet both reflect the influence of the Hebrew understanding of God
and his will for mankind.

For those whose interests are in history, the Old Testament becomes a significant source for primary data. The
documents of the "Father of History" are found in our
Bible (II Sam. 9–16, I Kings 1–2), not in the works of
Herodotus, the Greek historian. Insight into the causes of
wars among nations of antiquity may be found in the
library of our Bible. Among the great military leaders
referred to are Seti I, Ramses II, Mer-ne-Ptah, David,
Sheshak, Tiglath-pileser, Sargon, Sennacherib, Cyrus the
Great, Darius, Alexander the Great, and many others. Some
of the books of our biblical library state that all military
men and nations stand before the bar of God's judgment.

Readers whose disciplines are sociologically oriented find
in the Bible a basic source book for study of customs,
mores, and religious attitudes covering a thousand years.
Psychology of religion had its origin with Jeremiah's "Confessions." Philosophy of religion has been greatly aided by
expressions of Hebrew poetry such as Ps. 19, Job 38–39, and
Prov. 8:22-31, and so forth. Archaeologists find the begin-
nings of their science in biblical sites such as Jericho, Jerusalem, Bethshan, Megiddo, Hazor, Lachish, Joppa, Debir,
and so forth. Church musicians and those interested in
hymnody must begin with the pages of the Old Testament,
for in them are stored the insights of scores of persons
through the centuries who have searched for God and
found him. Their songs of doubt, of praise, of hope, of
sorrow, of certainty fill not only the hymnbooks but the
throats of thousands even today.

Besides those interested in the world's greatest literature,
in law, in sociology, in anthropology, in psychology of religion or in hymnody, we should add the discipline of com-
parative religions. The Old Testament is an excellent source
book for this discipline, for in it are found fragments from
the religious literature of the Sumerians, the Akkadians, the

Hittites, the Horites (Hurrians), the Egyptians, the Canaanites, the Philistines, the Persians, the Greeks, and the Romans, not to mention the Hebrews who carefully reworked many of these ancient rituals and much of the religious literature to make them become vehicles of Hebrew faith.

Undoubtedly the major value of the Old Testament for Christians is the faith of Israel which is embedded therein. The faith of Israel provided the Christian church with its basic tenets concerning the doctrine of God and the nature of God's self-revelation to man, the meaning of history and time, the nature of man and of the people of God. Let us note these briefly.

The apostle Paul's sermon at Antioch of Pisidia illustrates how the early Christian church appropriated the faith of the Old Testament and built the Christian church on it. A careful comparison of the old Confessional Creed of Deut. 26:5-9 and Josh. 24 with Acts 13:16-41 (Paul's sermon at Antioch) shows Paul's dependence on the former. Paul and the early church believed in common with Jews everywhere that: (a) "The God of this people Israel chose our fathers"; (b) "made the people great during their stay in the land of Egypt"; (c) "and with uplifted arm he led them out of it"; (d) "He bore with them in the wilderness"; (e) "He gave them their land as an inheritance"; and (f) "He raised up David to be their king." Paul added to the above creed, which he had memorized in his youth, a new point: (g) "Of this man's posterity God has brought to Israel a Savior, Jesus, as he promised." Clearly Paul built on the Hebrew faith of the God of the fathers, whose third promise to Abraham was finally fulfilled in Jesus: "And by you all the families of the earth will bless themselves" (Gen. 12:3b).

These confessional creeds emphasized the activity of God in and through the historical events in Israel's life. God's nature and will were made manifest through his gracious acts. From her experiences with the Lord who acted many times in Israel's behalf the people of Israel concluded that God was compassionate, loving, jealous (demanding that his people worship no other deity), just, and merciful.

God's will was made known in history, not only through acts of kindness in Israel's behalf but also in acts of judgment. If Israel were unfaithful, giving her loyalty to other deities (or governments, or things), then catastrophe fell upon her. The catastrophe could be in the form of war (as the fruit of national or international immoral living), or exile (as when Judah was taken into captivity in 587 B.C.), or severe tensions which came from estrangement from God and one's fellowmen. God's will was that Israel be loyal only unto him.

Through this concept of God's activity in history, Israel came into possession of a great gift: the knowledge that history has meaning. God was experienced as working out a plan, a purpose in history. He was seeking (as Amos taught) a people(s) whose national spirit would reflect kinship with his Spirit—a people whose individual lives and national policies would reflect compassion, justice, honor, mercy, love, and righteousness. Each person, each tribe, each clan, indeed each nation, had to choose whether it would work with God in his divine purpose in history, or rebel against him, and thus against itself, by denying his purpose. Whether the purposes of God and man agreed or not, God's purposes would prevail. Even so, the Lord yearned with a divine love that Israel and every nation might "seek the Lord and live."

History is thus viewed as the arena of God's activity; and historical events are seen as the media through which he reveals his will. For this reason the apostle Paul argued that God, who acted through Abraham, Moses, and David, was still active in Paul's day and, of course, he is active in our day too. One of the values of the Old Testament pertaining to our Christian faith is to make us face the question whether the Confessional Creeds of Deut. 26, Josh. 24, and Acts 13 are also our creeds—that is, do we really believe

that God was and is active in history? Is God a loving
Father, whose actions in history may be viewed sometimes as
catastrophe, sometimes as blessings or benedictions? The
question boils down to this: Do we believe God is active
in our history today? Paul and the Gospels would argue
that he is as active today as he was in the days of the
patriarchs and of his son Jesus Christ. Their faith moves
us to ask in what areas (historical events) is the Holy
Spirit moving today in behalf of his oppressed people
(modern Ninevites or Israelites) ?

Another tenet of Christian faith which is borrowed from
the Old Testament is the doctrine of man. It assumes the
creatureliness of man, a being who rebels from doing what
he knows is right, denies absolute standards, and stands
with pride and arrogance against God. The key to salvation is to respond by repentance, and turn in obedience
to his will.[1] The Old Testament view of man is not a
philosophical discussion of what "composes" man (flesh,
body, spiritual body, soul, and so forth) ; rather, it is concerned with man's relationship to God. The question is:
Does a man acknowledge what God has done for him, accept it with gratitude, and then move with obedience to
do the will of God? The real problem of life for one who
has acknowledged God's actions in his behalf is to *do* the
will of God, that is, to be obedient to his holy will.

For the Christian this means (if one acknowledges oneself as a part of the "New Israel," a participant in the
"New Covenant") that God has bound him to himself with
the good news of salvation (his great acts of love) and the
requirement of obedience (loyalty to his covenant). The
"tie that binds" is made of love, faith, and trust. Both
gospel and Law are involved, both promise and obedience.
Sin is then viewed as a betrayal of the divine love, as re-

---

[1] Paul and the Gospel of John take a different view from this. They assume
that man is so depraved by nature that he cannot even turn to God—only
God can do this. The synoptic gospels portray Jesus as steeped in the typical
Old Testament idea that man can turn to God through repentance—hence the
importance of preaching.

bellion or revolt against the Lordship of God. Such rebellion can be righted only by confession and forgiveness
and the joy of renewal of the covenant.

A man becomes his authentic self as he discovers who he
is—a child of God, a member of the New Israel, a participant of the New Covenant. For a Christian, the meaning
of life is found when one acknowledges the sovereignty of
God over his life, admits his creaturehood, and identifies his
life with the purposes of God as seen through the past
events of Israel's life. The purposes of God include the
sense of mission to be a "light for the Gentiles," a suffering servant through whom others might find the meaning
of existence as they learn that God is their Father, Creator,
Redeemer, and constant companion.

The Christian joins the Old Testament man in recognizing that with the bringing of proper things to the altar
a man worships God only when his inner attitude is right.
He who would worship in spirit and in truth must come
with an attitude of reverence, faith, trust, and love. So
taught Isaiah, Micah, Jeremiah, Deuteronomy, and others.

Perhaps we can learn something, too, from the Hebrew
custom of repeating the confessional creeds. The creeds
were basically recitals of what God had done in behalf of
Israel and in gratitude for his actions. Perhaps the New
Israel, the People of God, need to recapture a similar sense
of certainty. We need to ask if our creeds are personal recitals of what God has done *for us*. We need to learn to say
too: "Not with our fathers did the Lord make this covenant,
but with *us*, who are all of us here alive this day" (Deut.
5:3, italics added). Personal appropriation is essential; but
so also is the collective appropriation of the covenant. The
individual needs the community of faith (*koinonia*). The
Old Testament is basically a kerygmatic theme, centered in
the election of the fathers, salvation at the exodus, and
the gift of land in Canaan. The theme is true for Christians too—we have a proclamation (a kerygma) : God has
called ("chosen") us; he has redeemed us through Christ

from greed, pride, estrangement; he has offered us the promised land, the kingdom of God. Perhaps God is waiting as of old for a Caleb to say: "Let us go up at once, and possess [the land]." But having "possessed" the land the People of God are called upon to be a "kingdom of priests" to all people—to help those who know not the Lord to learn of him. The New Israel is a "light for the Gentiles" wherever any man lives in darkness. The New Israelite is to be a suffering servant that all men may know something of the love of God because of his compassionate suffering in man's behalf.

Hosea challenged Israel (and he challenges the New Israel) with the statement: "My people are destroyed for lack of knowledge" (Hos. 4:6a). The "knowledge" to which he referred did not mean information, but it referred to personal experience with God. To "know" God is to experience the deepest of personal relationships with the Lord of history. It is not enough to "know about" him. "Knowledge" is valid only when one is in right relationship with God's will. To have "knowledge" of God is to accept God's sovereignty and to trust that just as he has acted on behalf of Israel and the world in centuries past, so he is acting in history today to achieve the purposes for which he made our world. To "know" God is to accept him as Creator of the world, as Lord of history, as the totally "other" whose will is our salvation and our world's hope. To "know" God is to offer one's life in service to him, to be the means by which his will becomes incarnate, in every area of life (the economic, political, domestic, and international areas).

The essence of Christianity is the doctrine of the Incarnation. Basically it assures us that God entered human history in our behalf. Both Old and New Testaments vouch for this claim. God was and is and ever shall be active in history, working to achieve his purposes for his children. The crucifixion and God's resurrection of Jesus are for Christians the ultimate proof of the validity of this faith.

Appendix A

CHART OF BIBLICAL HISTORY

B.C.		PROPHETS
2000-1700	The Patriarchs: Abraham, Isaac, Jacob.	
1720-1580	Hyksos rule Egypt; Joseph Governor of Egypt.	
13th Century	Pharaoh Seti I oppresses children of Israel.	
	Ramses II, Pharaoh of Exodus.	
	Moses leads children of Israel out of Egypt, about 1260 B.C.	
	Joshua leads in conquest of Canaan, capturing Hazor, Lachish, and Bethel, about 1225 B.C.	
	Period of Judges.	
12th Century	Philistines find homeland in Canaan, about 1190 B.C.	Samuel
11th Century	Saul becomes first king of Hebrew clans, about 1015 B.C.	
10th Century	David is crowned king (1000 B.C.) Solomon, about 960-922 B.C.	Nathan
9th Century	Ahab and Jezebel.	Elijah Elisha
8th Century	Jeroboam II (Israel); Uzziah (Judah).	Amos Hosea
	Fall of northern kingdom, 721 B.C.	Isaiah Micah
7th Century	Josiah, and Deuteronomic Reform (621 B.C.)	Jeremiah
6th Century	Judah attacked twice by Nebuchadnezzar, 597, 587 B.C.	Ezekiel
	Cyrus the Great (Persian).	
	Building of Second Temple, 516 B.C.	Second Isaiah
5th Century		Nehemiah, Ezra
4th Century	Antiochus IV (Epiphanes).	

224

Appendix B

CHRONOLOGY OF LITERATURE

KEY DATES OF HISTORY—B.C.	LITERATURE
2000-1700 Patriarchs	
1260 Moses leads slaves out of Egypt	The Ten Commandments Song of Miriam
1200-1015 Period of Judges	Song of Deborah (Judges 5)
1000-960 David rules Monarchy ..	Possibly a few psalms Biography of King David
960-922 Solomon rules Monarchy..	The J tradition, about 930 B.C.
	Amos (760 B.C.) Hosea (747-735 B.C.) Isaiah (742-700 B.C.) E-traditions collected, about 730 B.C.
721 Fall of northern kingdom, Israel	(Possibly Deuteronomy?) Micah (about 701 B.C.) JE traditions about 660 B.C. Deuteronomy
621 Deuteronomic Reform under Josiah	Jeremiah Deuteronomy accepted as "Word of God," 621 B.C.
612 Fall of Nineveh (capital of Assyria)	Zephaniah, Nahum, Habakkuk
597, 587 Judah taken into exile in Babylonia	I, II Kings, about 600 B.C. Lamentations, 560 B.C. Ezekiel (593-571 B.C.) Job (580-540 B.C.) Joshua, Judges, Samuel, about 550 B.C.
538 Cyrus issues his decree	II Isaiah (40-55), 540-538 B.C. Haggai and Zechariah, 520-518 B.C.

KEY DATES OF HISTORY—B.C.   LITERATURE

516 Building of second temple in
Jerusalem ....   III Isaiah (56-66), 510 B.C.

                                   Obadiah, 460 B.C.
                                   Malachi, 460 B.C.
Artaxerxes I ....   Nehemiah, 460 B.C.
                                   I, II Chronicles, about 400 B.C.
                                   Ezra, about 400 B.C.

                                   Ruth, late 5th century B.C.
                                   The Priestly Code (P), 5th
                                   century B.C.
                                   The Psalms
                                   Jonah

                                   Joel, 400-350 B.C.
                                   Esther, 350 B.C.
333 Alexander the Great .... Proverbs
                                   Ecclesiastes, 250-200 B.C.
                                   Daniel
                                   Song of Songs

Index

Aaron, 30, 166
Abraham: chosen by God, 150, 154-57; historical background, 13-21; threefold promise to, 86, 89, 154, 159, 160
Absalom, 187
agriculture: *see* fertility deities
Ahab, 50-51
Ahaz, 54-55, 97
Ahimaaz, 81
Ahithophel, 187
Ai, 38
Akh-en-Aton, 26, 71, 159, 165
Akkadian culture, 14-18
Alexander the Great, 64
allegory, 149-50
Amorite culture, 18-20
Amos, 52, 89, 90-92, 94, 96-98, 189-92; book of, 72, 90-92, 199
Antiochus IV (Epiphanes), 65-66, 144
apocalyptic literature: Daniel, 142-46; Joel, 135; in Ezekiel, 142; in Isaiah, 142; in Zechariah, 124, 142
Aqabah, Gulf of, 83
Arameans, 19
Aristotle, 64
Ark of the Covenant, 33, 79-81, 133, 161, 170-72, 180, 181, 184, 186
Asherah, 42, 93, 101
Assyria, 51-53, 54-56, 99, 101, 107-8
Astarte, 42
Athaliah, 53, 67 n.

Baal, 42-43, 51, 101, 176, 178, 188-89
Babylonia, 14, 56, 57-61, 95, 107-8, 110-11, 113
Beersheba, 79, 156
Belshazzar, 59
Bethel, 38, 49-50, 80, 88-89, 90-92, 95, 119, 156, 180
Book of the Dead, 30, 168

camels, 41
Canaan: conquest of, 38-40, 86; culture of, 34, 36-37, 42-43, 69-70, 77-78, 93, 173; map, 29; promised land, 149, 154, 158, 160, 162, 175, 202
canon, 74-75
Chaldeans, 109
chariots, 15, 34, 39, 47, 51, 83, 108
cherubs, 171
chosen people, 150, 158-72, 206, 212-13
Chronicler, 211
Chronicles, books of, 75, 127-28, 151, 211
circumcision, 132
Commandments, Ten: *see* Ten Commandments
confederation of tribes, 35, 39-40; *see also* league of tribes
confessional creeds, 8-9, 19, 78, 79, 86, 88, 91, 106, 129, 150, 162, 175-78, 189, 219-20, 222
covenant: Book of the, 163; central theme of scripture, 7-10, 150; community, 118; Davidic, 128, 151, 181-87, 205, 208, 211; Mosaic, 150, 183, 208; new, 96, 112, 121-22, 151, 200-201, 202-4, 221-22; of Moses compared with Hittite treaties, 31-34; renewal of, 129, 150-52, 153, 164-65, 177, 210, 222; response to, 204; under Joshua, 39-40, 150-51, 153-54; with Abraham, 132, 150, 154-57
creation, 17, 70, 86, 133, 168
creeds, confessional: *see* confessional creeds
Cyrus, 59-62, 95, 123, 198

D (Deuteronomy), 73-74, 118-20, 163
Dan, 49-50, 88, 119
Daniel, book of, 65, 142-46

David, 45-47, 79-81, 84, 86-87, 98, 180, 182-84; see also covenant, Davidic
Deuteronomic Reform, 60, 105-7, 109-10, 185, 195-96
Deuteronomic writers, 91, 151, 183
Deuteronomy, 63, 72-73, 82, 105-7, 118-20, 129-30, 151, 163, 176-77, 194-97, 210
dispensations (eras) of human history, 132-33

E-tradition, 73-74, 82, 88-90, 102-3, 118-20, 154, 163, 170, 199
Ecclesiastes, 139-40
education: in Egypt (Moses), 25-26; in Ur (Abraham), 16; required of Jews, 67
Egypt, map, 29
Egyptian culture, 23, 24-27
El, 42, 70, 133
election, divine, 150-52, 153-57, 204, 212-13, 216
Elijah, 188-89
Elohim, 89
Ephraim, 73, 79 n.; see also Israel, northern kingdom
Esther, book of, 66, 136-37
exiles in Babylonia, 128, 130-31, 136
Exodus, 130, 163, 208, 210; second or new, 60, 96, 121-22, 202-3
Ezekiel, 59-60, 116-18, 174, 196, 200-201, 207; book of, 75, 116-18
Ezion-geber, 83
Ezra, 63, 123, 129-30, 140, 208, 209-10, 212; book of, 127, 128-30

fall, 17, 70, 86
family: in Ur, 17-18; intermarriage, 42, 63, 126, 129, 130, 212
Feast of Purim, 137
fertility deities, 84; in Canaan, 42-43, 93-94, 188-89; in Egypt, 30; in Ur, 17
festivals: lunar, 132; pilgrimage, 164-65, 178, 181, 183, 195
flood: Noah, 85, 132; Utnapishtim, 16, 70

Genesis, 85-86, 130
Gideon, 41

Gilgal, 79, 80, 90, 176, 180, 184
God: acting in history, 8-9, 71, 83-84, 106, 148-52, 220-21, 223; faith in, 116, 155-56; holiness of, 133; Incarnation, 223; kingdom of, 206-8; law of, 210-11; Lord of history, 87, 91, 136, 176, 190; name of, 42; nature of, 194, 219-20; of justice, 90-92, 94, 108, 190; of love, 92-94, 104-5, 108; personal relationship to, 213-16, 223; providence of, 155, 163; saving acts of, 148-52, 158-72, 179; sovereignty of, 133; transcendence of, 117, 140, 167; will of, 169, 172, 192, 213, 220; word of, 208; see also Yahweh
Greek culture, 64, 139

Habakkuk, book of, 108-9
Haggai, 62, 123-24; book of, 123-24
Hammurabi, 16, 20, 168
Hanukkah, 66, 145
Haran, 18, 70, 85
Hasidim, 66, 144-45
Hazor, 39
Hebron, 22, 45, 156
Hellenistic culture, 64-65
Herod the Great, 67
historian, court, under David, 46
History: Father of, 81, 218; in Old Testament, 218; meaning of, 71, 220; salvation-history, 12, 149, 183 n.; theology of, 91, 150-52, 198-99; two approaches, 11-12, 148
Hittites, treaties, 31-34
Holiness Code, 129
Hosea, 52, 92-94, 96-98, 174, 176, 192; book of, 82, 92-94
Hurrian culture, 20-21
Hyksos culture, 22-23

individual responsibility, 213-16
inheritance customs, 20-21, 51
intermarriage, 42, 63, 126, 129, 130, 212
Isaac, 155-56
Isaiah, 54-56, 77, 95-98, 192-93

Isaiah 40–55, writer of: see Second Isaiah

Isaiah 56–66, writer of: see Third Isaiah

Isaiah, book of, 75, 90; Chapters 1–39, 95-98; Chapters 40–55, 95-96, 120-22; Chapters 56–66, 96, 123, 125

Israel, name of, 178

Israel, new, 122, 221-23

Israel, northern kingdom, 50-53, 90, 91-92, 94, 95-98

Israel, people: as chosen people, 150; uniqueness of, 71

Israel, united kingdom, 43-48

J-document, 82-87, 89-90, 102-3, 154; writer of, 46, 82; see also Yahwist

J-tradition, 73-74, 118-20, 156, 163, 199

Jabesh-gilead, 44

Jacob, 84, 89, 156; historical background, 19-21

Jamnia, Council of, 75, 134, 139

JE, 73, 102-3, 118-20, 154, 199

JED, 118-20

JEDP, 74

Jehoiachin, 58-59

Jehu, 51-52

Jeremiah, 56, 58-59, 104-5, 109-12, 174, 196; book of, 75, 104-5, 109-12

Jericho, conquest of, 38

Jeroboam I, 48, 49-50, 79, 88

Jeroboam II, 52, 54, 88, 90, 95

Jerusalem, 45, 47, 56, 59-61, 66-67, 80, 95-96, 98, 107, 110, 118-20, 180, 184, 186; destruction of, 57, 111, 113-14, 198; New, 118, 201; rebuilding, 62-63, 129

Jesus, 67, 204

Jethro, 158, 160

Jezebel, 50-51, 53, 93

Job, book of, 115-16, 143 n., 217

Joel, 135-36; book of, 64, 135-36

Jonah, book of, 66, 75, 140-42, 212-13

Joseph, 84, 156-57; historical background, 21-23; "house of," 24, 35, 40

Joshua, 35, 36-40, 150-51, 154, 175-78; book of, 75, 119-20, 175-78

Josiah, 195-96

Judah, southern kingdom, 53-56, 73, 99, 101-2

Judaism, 210-11

Judges, 179; book of, 75, 91, 119-20; nature of, 40-43

Kadesh-barnea, 34-35, 173

king, responsibilities of, 185

kingdom of God, 206-8

Kings, books of, 75, 81, 82, 84, 91, 118

Koheleth, 139

Lamech, 76, 85

Lamentations, 113-14

law: birthright, 21; books of, 74-75, 210-11; Canaanite, 69; Code of Ur-Nammu, 15; Egyptian, 30; in Old Testament, 217; inheritance customs, 20-21, 51; Mesopotamian, 30; Mosaic, 63, 129-30, 133, 163-69; of Ezra, 63

league of tribes, 154, 175-79

legalism, 133, 195-96, 211

Leviticus, 130, 208, 210

Maccabean revolt, 65-67, 145

Malachi, book of, 126-27

man, doctrine of, 221

Manasseh, 101-3

map, 29

Mari, 18

Mesopotamia, 14

Messiah, 60, 62, 95, 98, 182, 204, 211

Micah, 56, 99-100, 193; book of, 99-100

minor prophets, books of, 75

monarchy: rise of, under Saul, 43-45; under David, 45-47; under Solomon, 47-48

Moses: covenant maker, 28-34, 150; deliverer, 27-28, 161-62; historical background, 24-35, 159-60; Law of, 129-30; meaning of name, 185; relation to Deuteronomy, 106; religious experience, 158-61

Nabonidus, 59
Naboth, 51
Nahum, book of, 107-8
Nathan, 151, 154, 182-83, 185-86
nationalism: of Esther, 137; of Nahum, 107-8; of Obadiah, 125-26
Nebuchadnezzar, 57-59
Nehemiah, 62-63, 123, 128-29, 140, 208, 209, 212; book of, 127, 128-30
New Testament, covenant in, 151
Nineveh, 107-8, 141, 212
Numbers, 130, 163, 208, 210
Nuzi, 20

Obadiah, book of, 125-26
obedience to the Law, 61, 128, 221
Omri, 50

P-document, 73-74, 163; *see also* Priestly Code
Passover, 132
patriarchs, 13-23, 150-57
Paul, 68, 94, 98, 219
Pentateuch, 63, 65, 74, 129-30, 140, 150, 210
persecution, 136-37, 146
Persian empire, 61-64
Pfeiffer, Robert H., 81
Pharisee, meaning of, 136
Phariseeism, 133
Pharisees, 66-67, 197
Philistines, 37, 43-44, 54-55, 82
pilgrimage festivals, 164-65, 178, 181, 183, 195
poetry: acrostic, 114; Job, 115-16; parallelism, 42
prayer, 214-16; Abraham, 156; exiles, 131; Jeremiah, 111-12
priesthood, meaning of, 204
Priestly Code, 74, 129, 130-33, 170-71, 206-9, 210-11
Priestly writers, 131
priests, duties of, 184
prophecy, relation to written scripture, 142, 196
Prophets, books of, canonized, 74-75
prophets, eighth-century, 188-94
Proverbs, book of, 66, 75, 137-39

Psalms, book of, 66, 75, 131, 134-35, 186, 214
Ptolemaic empire, 64
Purim, Feast of, 137

Rachel, 20
Ramses II, 24-27, 162; meaning of name, 185
Rehoboam, 48, 49, 54, 79
religion: Babylonian, 15-17; Egyptian (Akh-en-Aton), 26, 165; imageless, 160-61, 166-67; in Proverbs, 138; Persian, 62, 143; personal, 111-12, 213-16
repentance, 120, 141, 221
Ruth, 130; book of, 75, 130, 141, 212-13, 217

Sabbath, 132, 168
sacrifice, human, 101
sacrificial system, 132, 191
Sadducees, 66-67
salvation-history, 12, 149, 183 n.
salvation: Israel's concept of, 153; key to, 221
Samaria, 50, 53, 79 n.
Samaritans, 53, 63, 67
Samuel, 44-45, 180, 181-82; books of, 75, 81, 82, 91, 119-20, 183
Sargon II, 52-53, 55
Satan, 143 n.
Saul, 43-45, 79, 84, 181-82
Second Isaiah, 59-60, 77, 120-22, 141, 196, 202-4, 207-8
Seleucid empire, 64
Sennacherib, 55
Septuagint, 65
Seti I, 24-27, 158
Shalmaneser, 52
Shechem: Abraham's altar, 21, 107 154, 156; covenant renewal, 164-65, 176, 210; covenant under Joshua, 39-40, 107, 151, 153, 177-78, 210; creeds of, 78, 86, 129; home of Leah tribes, 24, 35, 177; Jeroboam's capital, 88; tribal shrine, 79, 89, 91, 184
Shiloh, 44, 79, 180, 181, 184
Sinai, 28-30, 42, 158-59, 162-69; map, 29
slavery in Egypt, 26-27

Solomon, 47-48, 79, 82-87; wisdom of, 82-83
Song of Songs, 77, 146-47
songs, early, 76-77
sources of Old Testament, 74
storytellers, early, 70
study, methods of, 72, 149
suffering servant, 96, 120, 133, 204, 222-23
Sumerian culture, 14-18
synagogue, 60-61, 131
Syria, 54-55

tabernacle, 163
temple: Ezekiel's idea of, 60, 118, 201, 207; Herod's, 61, 67; of Elephantine Jews, 61, 63; Second, 62, 65, 123-24, 144, 205; Solomon's, 47, 55-56, 60, 85, 96, 98, 110-11, 184, 191, 198
Ten Commandments, 77, 132, 163-69, 171
tent of meeting, 163, 169-71
Terah, 16, 18-19
teraphim, 20
Third Isaiah, 123, 125
Tiglath-pileser III, 52, 54
Torah, 65, 68, 74, 184-85

treaties: Hittite, 31-34, 169; of Solomon, 47-48

Ur of the Chaldeans, 14-18, 70, 84
Urim and Thummim, 171, 184
Uzziah, 54, 95

Weidner, Ernst, 58
wilderness experience, 174-75
wisdom literature, 137-39, 139-40
worship: in Amos' view, 91; ritual given at Sinai, 133
writings, canonization of, 75

Yahweh, 70, 71, 101, 120-22, 131, 142-43, 145; at Sinai, 162; at the Reed Sea, 161-62; covenant with Israel, 30; in Canaan, 42-43, 176; Jeroboam's idea of, 50; meaning of, 160; name of, 73, 132, 160-61, 167; personal relationship with, 213-16
Yahwist, 82-87, 89

Zechariah, 62, 123-24; book of, 64, 123-24
Zephaniah, book of, 103-4
Zerubbabel, 62, 123-24, 205
ziggurat, 15-17, 85

DATE DUE

JE 26 87			
JY 0 67			
JY 10 67			
JY 13 67			
OC 19 67			
MAR 03 '80			
	WITHDRAWN FROM		
	OHIO NORTHERN		
	UNIVERSITY LIBRARY		
GAYLORD			PRINTED IN U.S.A.